I0160109

Rhyming Stories

language workbook

Susan Boyer

© Boyer Educational Resources 2014

Published in Australia by Boyer Educational Resources
for worldwide distribution.
www.boyereducation.com.au
Phone/fax: + 61 2 4739 1538

Copyright laws allow for a maximum of one chapter (or 10%) of this book to be copied by educational institutions for educational purposes **provided** that the educational institution has given a remuneration notice to the copyright agency of that country.

Enquiries for copying for any other purpose should be made to the publisher.
No part of this publication may be reproduced, stored in a retrieval system
or transmitted in any form or by any means electronic, mechanical, photocopying, recording or otherwise, without the prior consent of the publisher.

National Library of Australia Cataloguing-in-Publication

Boyer, Susan Elizabeth

Rhyming stories – language workbook

ISBN: 978 1 877074 06 6

421.52 English language – Spelling – Pronunciation

See accompanying story book & audio CD for English language and literacy practice:

Rhyming stories – practice with the sounds and spelling of English .... ISBN 978 1 877074 06 6
Rhyming stories – audio CD... ISBN 978 1 877074 37 0

Cover design by Susan Boyer
Acknowledgments, see page 106.

© Boyer Educational Resources 2014

Boyer Educational Resources
PO Box 255, Glenbrook, 2773, Australia,
Phone/Fax + 61 2 4739 1538

Cover images

From left to right: marble carver by Susan Boyer; woman blowing bubbles from Microsoft; man in kayak by Susan Boyer; student with blue background purchased from Fotolia; man in bookstore purchased from photos.com; waitress in coffee shop purchased from photo.com; woman with golden roses by Susan Boyer; chef purchased from Fotolia; painter at easel purchased from photos.com; man looking at painting by Susan Boyer

ABOUT THIS BOOK

'*Rhyming Stories - language workbook*' has been developed to provide complementary learning activities for '*Rhyming Stories - practice with the sounds and spelling of English*'(A5 storybook). An audio recording of *Rhyming Stories* is also part of this learning resource.

The activities have been designed so that students can work through them in class with other students, or alone, without the help of a teacher. The language exercises were developed to provide reinforcement of English spelling patterns introduced through each of the stories in '*Rhyming Stories - practice with the sounds and spelling of English*'.

Each story (in the storybook) focuses on a particular sound of English as well as telling a narrative on a different topic. Therefore, each corresponding section of this language workbook focuses on the same sound and its spelling variations. It also includes additional activities to extend the topic while providing repetition through listening, speaking, reading and writing on the theme of the story.

For example, the language activities for '**Jen the apprentice chef**', focus on and provide reinforcement of spelling variations for the sound /e/, but also provide explanation and practice on 'how to use a dictionary' and speaking activities on the topic of food and cooking.

Each unit of this 'language workbook' is divided into different sections, which explain and provide practice with various aspects of English spelling and pronunciation in a systematic and enjoyable way:

- Each unit begins with a **vocabulary or word matching activity** which focuses on the meaning of words found in each specific story. The activity aims to familiarise learners with the meaning of words they will use in later exercises . It also emphasises the link between English sounds and spelling, as the words in the matching activity have the focus sound of that corresponding story.

- After the matching activity, learners are required to write the answers into a crossword which consolidates spelling patterns.

- The subsequent activity comprises simple comprehension questions about the story to ensure readers engage with the topic while practising language features.

- Next, learners are required to **listen and read the story and write the missing words** (all of which contain the focus sound of that story) into the text. This process draws attention to the spelling variations of the focus sound of that particular story.

- A short activity follows in which learners identify one word with a different sound to other words on the same line. Answers to these exercises are provided at the back of this book.

- Various additional activities follow which include researching or speaking on a topic through surveys and/or discussion. Other activities include analysing language features of English, such as 'silent letters', homophones and particular letter combinations common in English.

- Each unit also contains an activity where learners write words into lists (according to their sound - spelling correlation). The completed lists can be checked against the 'Spelling Reference Lists' at the back of '*Rhyming Stories – practice with the sounds and spelling of English*' (A5 storybook).

                                                    © Boyer Educational Resources

Dear 'Rhyming Stories' user,

This book has been designed to help you to understand the link between English sounds and spelling, and to provide fun activities that will help you to improve your spelling. This book will provide the most benefit when used with the accompanying storybook, *'Rhyming stories – practice with the sounds and spelling of English'* and the audio recording.

Some central points to know about English spelling and pronunciation:

o   <u>Twenty-six letters</u> are used to write English.

o   <u>Forty sounds</u> are used in spoken English.

o   Since there are **more sounds** in spoken English than **letters** in written English, some **letters represent more than one sound**.

The rhyming stories in this book range from 150 to 250 words and each contains a simple story that focuses on a specific **sound** of English. Every story is illustrated with visual cues and colours which also help to demonstrate the link between the sounds and spelling of English words.

When learning any new skill it is important to realise that there is more than one method that can be helpful. This book contains a variety of learning activities aimed at improving spelling. For example, this book encourages the use of all the following skills and senses:

o   visual – **seeing** and identifying the spelling patterns and their relationship to pronunciation by reading the 'Rhyming Stories'

o   auditory – **hearing** and recognising words with the same sound in each 'Rhyming Story' on the audio recording

o   physical – **writing** words with the focus sound with its spelling combinations helps us remember patterns; for example, completing the spelling lists in this book for each 'Rhyming Story'. (Also see information about 'English Vowel Sound Spelling Charts' below.)

o   verbal - **saying** words aloud as we consciously focus on the spelling also helps to implant the pattern in our mind.

o   logical – **understanding** the limited spelling patterns of English, such as which letter combinations are possible and which combinations never occur in English.

The approach used in this book also recognises that **repetition** is central to learning, particularly with improving spelling. Most importantly, the approach takes into account that successful learning happpens best when we **enjoy what we are doing**. Therefore, my aim with this book is to provide stories that are varied, interesting and fun.

PDF versions of *'English Vowel Sound Spelling Charts'* (colour and/or illustrated) can be purchased, downloaded and printed to any size appropriate for your classroom or learning space.

See: www.englishebooks.com

The charts can be laminated and re-used multiple times for students to write words according to their spelling variations on the matching coloured chart as a lasting visual 'ready-reckoner'.

A4 size laminated *'English Vowel Sound Spelling Charts'* can be bought at:

www.boyereducation.com.au

Suggestions for students working through this course independently:

➢ Improving your spelling is all about repetition, so the more you do, the easier it will become.

➢ Reading and listening to stories at the same time is a very effective way to become familar with the spelling patterns of English.

➢ After listening to a story, try reading it aloud. This will help you focus on the spelling as well as the sounds contained in the words.

➢ Write new or difficult words onto small 'word cards' that you can carry in your pocket or wallet. Use time waiting in queues or for appointments to memorise the spelling of new words, then check the cards to see if you got the spelling right.

➢ You may need to check the meaning of some new words in a dictionary, so have a good dictionary nearby while you are studying. Because English words are not always pronounced as they are spelt, you may also need to use a dictionary to learn the correct pronunciation.

➢ It helps to be familiar with words and expressions used to talk about spelling and pronunciation and to understand what dictionary symbols mean. A list of words relating to spelling and language learning is given on page 6 of *Rhyming Stories – practice with the sounds and spelling of English*. Also, an explanation and practice in using a dictionary is given on page 11 of this workbook.

➢ If you are also focusing on the pronunciation of English words, mark the stress patterns of words on the same cards so that you can say the words correctly. See pages 5, 9 and 11 of this book for an explanation and practice with understanding 'word stress'.

➢ When using this book with the audio recording, practise saying the new words aloud. Record your voice so that you can check your pronunciation.

➢ Practise writing in English every day. Try to use the new words you have learnt in your writing.

➢ Remember, improving your spelling is like success in any new skill: the more you do it, the easier it will become!

Rhyming Stories – language workbook

Contents

Rhyming Stories – language workbook

Contents

© Boyer Educational Resources

Rhyming Stories – language workbook

Contents

© Boyer Educational Resources

Rhyming Stories – language workbook

Contents

Rhyming Stories – Language activities for 'Dan's Black Hat Jazz Band'
Words with the same vowel sound as in 'black'

Write the words in the box next to their meaning, then write them in the crossword

valued	black	band	jazz	fantastic	cap	plan	fan
tap	fact	van ✓	banjo	talent	clap	saxophone (also called 'sax')	

1. a road vehicle used for carrying things   -   _____ van _____

2. thought to be important, of value, appreciated   -   _____

3. the darkest colour   -   _____

4. a person who likes and admires a famous person   -   _____

5. a group of musicians who play music together   -   _____

6. information that you know is true   -   _____

7. a metal instrument that makes music by blowing with the mouth   -   _____

8. very good, excellent   -   _____

9. a soft flat hat, sometimes with an eye-shade section at the front   -   _____

10. a type of music with a strong lively beat   -   _____

11. an idea of what you are going to do   -   _____

12. a musical instrument like a guitar but with a round body   -   _____

13. to hit something gently with one hand or finger   -   _____

14. a natural skill or ability to do something   -   _____

15. hit your hands together to show you enjoyed something   -   _____

Answers, page 81.

Read and listen to the story about 'Dan's Black Hat Jazz Band'.
Comprehension questions:

1. What kind of music does Dan play? _____

2. What do Dan, Jack and Max wear when they play in their band? _____

3. What do people do when they hear the band?_____

Listen to the rhyming story again.

Write in the missing words with the same vowel sound as 'bl<u>a</u>ck':

Dan is a musical _____

who always has a_____,

and one of the talents he _____,

is to play fantastic _____!

Dan has a friend called Max

who plays the banjo and _____.

So they got together and _____

the 'Black Hat Jazz _____'.

Dan has a friend called Jack

who drives a van that's _____.

The van is great for the_____,

as they travel round the _____.

They pack all their things in the _____

with a black hat for each _____.

The band's well known for its _____

but also, for the style it _____.

When the men appear in their hats or _____

people stand and everyone_____!

They're most valued with their _____

for the music they make with their _____

Wherever they play round the _____

people tap out the beat with their_____.

It's a fact well known by the _____,

that music's a language we all _____!

Spelling and pronunciation practice

One word in each line doesn't have the same vowel sound as 'bl_a_ck'? Circle the different word.

If you are not sure, check the pronunciation of the words in your dictionary.

1.	v_a_n	m_a_n	pl_ay_s	b_a_nd
2.	t_a_ll	fl_a_t	bl_a_ck	h_a_t
3.	h_a_s	j_a_zz	l_a_nd	c_a_ll
4.	f_a_ns	m_a_ke	h_a_nd	cl_a_p

Speaking activity 1
Ask three people the following questions and write 'one or two word' answers.

Survey questions	Name:	Name:	Name:
1. What kind of music do you like?			
2. Who is your favourite musician or musical band?			
3. Can you play a musical instrument?			
4. Which musical instrument would you like to learn to play?			

Speaking activity 2
Dan had a plan to form a jazz band; that was his 'ambition'.
An ambition is something you want to do in your life. What is **your** ambition?
Talk about an ambition you have and how you plan to accomplish that ambition?

Speaking activity 3 Discuss your idea about what the following sentence means?

'Music's a language we all understand'.

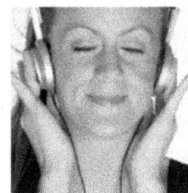

Pronunciation practice – syllables   (Answers, page 81.)

Spoken words are made with syllables, or units of sound. Each syllable contains a vowel sound.
For example: 'come' has one syllable; 'welcome' has two syllables; 'unwelcome' has three syllables.

Look at the following words from the story about 'Dan's Black Hat Jazz Band'.
Decide how many syllables each word contains and write the word in the correct column below.

black	band	fantastic music hat plan fans banjo	
talent	travel	people clap saxophone understand	

one syllable	two syllables	three syllables

Understanding English Pronunciation

Word Stress

In English words with two or more syllables, one of the syllables is spoken more strongly than the other syllables.

- The strong syllables are known as *stressed* syllables.
- The weak syllables are known as *unstressed* syllables.

In the following words, the first syllable is stronger than the second syllable.

talent
banjo   The stressed (strong) syllable is **bold**.
travel

In the following words, the second syllable is stronger than the first syllable.

ap**pear** The stressed (strong) syllable is **bold**.
fan**tas**tic

Sentence stress

In spoken English we **stress** the words which give the most important information in a sentence. This means the important words are stronger and louder. This is similar to the beat in music.

In music, some sounds are l o n g and **loud**;
some sounds are short and soft.

For example, in the sentence below the stressed words are: **Dan** – **friend** – **Jack** – **drives** – **van** – **black**
Read the sentence aloud and clap on the stressed words

Dan has a **friend** called **Jack**

who **drives** a **van** that's **black**.

This pattern of strong and weak stress is like the beat in music and gives us the rhythm of English.

When words in a sentence have more than one syllable, we put the stress on only the stressed part, not the whole word. In the example sentence below, there are four words with more than one syllable.
These words are: **mu**sical – **al**ways – **tal**ents – fan**ta**stic

Read the sentence aloud and clap on the stressed words or the stressed syllables .

Dan is a **mu**sical **man**

who **al**ways **has** a **plan**,

and **one** of the **tal**ents he **has**,

is to **play** fan**ta**stic **jazz**!

Listen to 'Dan's Black Hat Jazz Band' rhyming story again and mark the sentence stress.
The stress and rhythm of 'Dan's Black Hat Jazz Band' is shown on page 44-45 of 'Rhyming Stories' storybook.

Most dictionaries show stress in words with the mark '
before (or after) the stressed syllable.

Some dictionaries underline the stressed syllable.

Check the 'Pronunciation Guide' in your dictionary to see how word stress is shown.

Rhyming Stories – Language activities for 'Jen, the apprentice chef'
Words with the same vowel sound as in 'red'

Write the words in the box next to their meaning, then write them in the crossword.

chef	apprentice✓	suspect	deaf	yelled	went	stressed	instead
upset	said	many	excel	seven	guess	test	fresh

1. an experienced cook who prepares food in a restaurant   -   _____

2. a person who works for a period of time to learn a skill   -   ____apprentice____

3. unable to hear   -   _____

4. worried and not able to relax   -   _____

5. one more than six   -   _____

6. unhappy about something   -   _____

7. think(something) may be true   -   _____

8. shouted words loudly   -   _____

9. think about what the answer or result may be   -   _____

10. in the place of something else   -   _____

11. past verb of 'go'   -   _____

12. past verb of 'say'   -   _____

13. be very good at doing something   -   _____

14. recently made, not old   -   _____

15. an examination or questions to check knowledge or ability   -   _____

16. a large number or amount of something   -   _____

Answers, page 82.

Read and listen to the story about 'Jen, the apprentice chef'.

Comprehension questions:

1. What did Jen not suspect about her health? _____

2. What did Jen give Jeff when he asked for seven eggs? _____

3. What did Jen do when Jeff said he thought she was deaf? _____

4. What was the result of Jen's next cooking test? _____

Listen to the rhyming story again.

Write the missing words with the same vowel sound as 'red':

Jen's an apprentice _____

who works with a man called _____.

A problem she didn't _____

is that she's a little bit _____.

When Jeff said to start at seven,

Jen arrived at ten to_____.

When Jeff yelled and shook his _____.

Jen didn't get what he'd _____.

In the kitchen, where everything's _____

Jen excelled at making _____.

She always did her _____

but Jeff kept getting _____.

Jeff knew she was trying her _____

so one day he gave her a _____.

When he said to get seven eggs

she thought he said chicken _____!

When he said to get fresh _____,

she collected red pens _____.

'Now don't get upset' said _____,

'but I think you're a little bit_____.'

So Jen went and had many _____

and now does as the doctor _____.

When Jen took her next cooking _____,

as always, she did her_____.

When all the marks were _____,

and ready for Jen to _____,

The result was as you've _____:

Jen had done better than all the _____!

Spelling and pronunciation practice

One word in each line <u>doesn't</u> have the same vowel sound as 'red'? Circle the different word.

1.	deaf	hear	get	stressed
2.	chef	went	her	test
3.	he	ten	fresh	eggs
4.	seven	red	pens	please

Speaking activity 1

Ask three people the following questions and write 'one word' answers.

Survey questions	Name:	Name:	Name:
1. What is your favourite food?			
2. What food do you never eat?			
3. What is your favourite recipe?			

Speaking activity 2

Form a small group and share a recipe in which the **main ingredient** is **egg**:

or

a vegetable

or

lemons

Tell your group all the ingredients in your recipe and explain the method (how you make it).

The following verbs will be helpful:

chop	grate	beat	boil	fry	bake

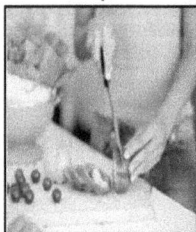     

Spelling and pronunciation - homophones

Some pairs of English words have the **same pronunciation** but a **different spelling pattern** and meaning.
These words are called homophones, meaning 'same sound'
For example, '**bread**' means 'a type of food' and '**bred**' means 'produced animals for a particular farming purpose'.
These words have the same pronunciation but are spelt differently.

Put the words '**bread**' and '**bred**' in the correct place in the following sentence:

On the farm, we_____ sheep for wool and cows for milk. We also made our own _____.

Further practice

Choose the correct word (from the choice given for each sentence) and complete the sentences.
Use your dictionary if necessary. (**Answers, page 82.**)

guest/guessed

1. Have you _____ who is going to be the special _____ at the party tonight?

red/read

2. Yesterday he _____ every story in the book with the _____ cover.

sent/scent

3. My friend _____ me a birthday card and some expensive _____ in a beautiful bottle.

weather/whether

4. The TV report didn't show _____ tomorrow's _____ will be hot or cold!

Pronunciation practice - word stress

In English words with two or more syllables, one of the syllables is usually spoken more strongly than the other syllables. This is called 'word stress'. If you put the stress on the wrong syllable you can change the meaning of the word.

Some English words with the same spelling can have more than one meaning. For example, some words can be used to mean a thing, place or an emotion (a noun); the same word can mean an action (a verb). The written word may look the same but the pronunciation may be different.

Look at the focus words in the sentences below and notice the stress patterns.
The stressed (strong) syllables are **bold** and <u>underlined</u>.

Word -	as a noun	as a verb
↓	↓	↓
upset	We had an **up**set at work today.	My friend up**set** a customer.
suspect	She is a **sus**pect for the theft.	We sus**pect** she stole the money.
present	My birthday **pre**sent was lovely.	I'll pre**sent** the certificates today.
desert	A **de**sert is a hot dry place.	We'll de**sert** the town if the flood comes.

Can you see a pattern?

> **Nouns** are generally stressed on the **first** syllable; **verbs** are generally stressed on the **second** syllable. However, this is a guide only. You can use your dictionary to check the pronunciation of new words.

Spelling lists – Words with the short vowel sound in 'red'

- Write words from **Jen's** story with the short vowel sound in the word **red**.
  (There are more than 30 words)
- Put words in the correct column according to its spelling pattern. Then you can compare your list with the 'Spelling Reference Lists' at the back of the '**Rhyming Stories**' storybook.

e	ea	a
apprentice	deaf	many

Also: *said, guessed*

Write words for things illustrated on the **red** picture page (p. 10) with the short sound in **red**.
There are more than 15 words.

e	ea	a
Jen	breakfast	many
restaurant		

Using a dictionary to help understand the sounds and spelling of English

As you have seen on the previous page, the sounds of English can be written with different letter combinations. Therefore, it is helpful to know that your dictionary can help you.

Dictionaries use symbols to represent the sounds of English so that you can see a written word and know how to pronounce it correctly. A <u>symbol</u> is a <u>sign</u> used to represent something.

The information below explains what the different marks and symbols in a dictionary mean.

Checking pronunciation in a dictionary

The pronunciation of a word is shown in dictionaries between diagonal lines / / and the <u>pronunciation</u> of the word is usually shown <u>before its meaning</u> and an example of the word is given. So, if you check the word 'seven' in a dictionary, it will look something like this:

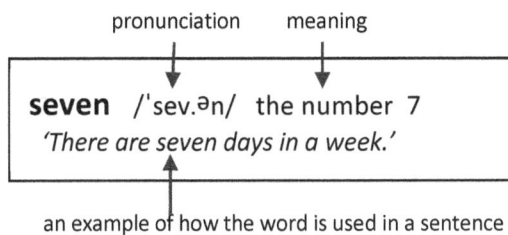

pronunciation   meaning

seven /ˈsev.ən/ the number 7
'There are seven days in a week.'

an example of how the word is used in a sentence

Dictionary sound symbols

Sometimes the letters of the English alphabet, and their dictionary sound symbols are the same.
For example, if you check the word 'red' in a dictionary, the pronunciation will generally be shown as /red/.
In other words, the letters 'r', 'e' and 'd' in *red* are the same as the sound symbols that show how to say '*red*'.
(Some dictionaries use the symbol ɛ in /rɛd/ to represent the vowel sound 'e' in the word red, but it is less common.)

However, because there are more English sounds than letters, other symbols are used to represent English sounds. A list of 'English pronunciation symbols' is usually at the beginning or end of a dictionary. You can also find information about this online. It is not necessary to learn every sound symbol but it is useful to know where to find help if you need to check the pronunciation of an word.

Other dictionary symbols

- The division of syllables is usually shown by a dot between syllables as in /ˈsev.ən/, which has two syllables.
- The main stress in words is shown as in the example word above with a mark ', like an apostrophe.
- The symbol ə (called 'schwa') is an international symbol used to represent a short, quiet sound used in many English words. Look again at the above dictionary example for 'seven'. It shows that the second part of the word (the second syllable) should be quicker and quieter than the first.

Dictionary practice

As an example, check the word 'welcome' in your dictionary. How is the pronunciation shown?

_____

In many dictionaries, the word '**welcome**' is shown as /ˈwelkəm/. The symbol /ə/ in the word 'welcome', tells a dictionary reader to pronounce the second part of the word more quickly and quietly than the first part of the word.

The sound symbols used in many dictionaries are called the 'International Phonetic Alphabet'(IPA). Not **all** dictionaries use these symbols so check which symbols your dictionary uses.

You can learn more about the pronunciation of English and using the 'International Phonetic Alphabet' in: '*Understanding English Pronunciation'*. See back cover for details.

Rhyming Stories – Language activities for 'Some bubble-gum fun'

Words that have the same vowel sound as in 'some fun'

Write the words in the box next to their meaning, then write them in the crossword

adult	young	bubble✓	gum	a must	fuss	tough	troubles	hum
stuff	encourage	hub	gruff	customs	club	glum		

1. a ball of air or gas inside a thin covering of liquid or gum   -   <u>   bubble   </u>

2. soft, sticky elastic material (often found in trees or plants)   -   _____

3. not old   -   _____

4. speak in a way that gives someone confidence to do something   -   _____

5. something that is necessary   -   _____

6. a place that is the centre of an activity   -   _____

7. a fully grown person   -   _____

8. to make a tune or music without opening your mouth   -   _____

9. unhappy or sad   -   _____

10. an organisation for people who want to share a social activity   -   _____

11. this word can mean 'things', 'thoughts' or 'ideas'   -   _____

12. habits, traditions or ways of behaving   -   _____

13. worry or anxiety about unimportant things   -   _____

14. problems   -   _____

15. difficult, unfair, not easy ('rough' can have a similar meaning)   -   _____

16. unfriendly   -   _____

Answers, page 83.

Read and listen to the story about 'Some bubble-gum fun'.
Comprehension questions:

1. Where do Justin and Honey live? _____

2. What did Justin's mum say he <u>didn't</u> need to have fun?_____

3. What did Honey and Justin's mum encourage them to start? _____

4. What was the purpose of the 'Bubble-gum Hub? _____

Listen to the rhyming story again.

Write in the missing words with the same vowel sound as 'bubble':

Justin and Honey are young <u>adults</u>.

who've studied hard for great _____.

Justin is Honey's younger_____;

they both live with their father and_____.

They're clever, smart, young and _____

but between them both there's not much_____.

They don't have a car so they catch the _____

and live their lives without much_____.

A sensible mother is their _____,

always reminding her daughter and _____:

'You don't need much money to have great_____.'

Their mother's life had at times been _____

but they'd never seen her angry or_____.

She's an optimist, when times get_____;

She has her family and that's_____.

When Justin's down and feeling <u>glum</u>

she comes up with stuff that can be _____.

'Enjoy outdoors when the weather's_____,

relax, breathe deep, just don't _____.

Swim and ride and jump and_____.

It doesn't matter what your age is _____!

Do simple things to forget your _____;

like hum a song or blow some _____!'

She encouraged the youngsters to set up a_____,

which they did, and called it the 'Bubble-gum_____'.

Among friends of all cultures, the club is a_____.

Sharing customs and music, so much is _____!

At the end of the day, what the club's mostly_____,

is show simple things are the ultimate _____.

Spelling and pronunciation practice
One word in each line <u>doesn't</u> have the same vowel sound as 'b<u>u</u>bble'? Circle the different word.

If you are not sure, check the pronunciation of the words in your dictionary.

1.	young	your	tough	rough
2.	song	some	stuff	gum
3.	come	some	both	done
4.	run	do	jump	hum

Answers, page 83.

Speaking activity 1
Ask three people the following questions and write 'one or two word' answers.

Survey questions	Name:	Name:	Name:
1. Can you blow bubbles with gum?			
2. Are you a member of any clubs? (book club, sports club, community group)			
3. What simple things do you do to have fun?			

Speaking activity 2 - Group task

Imagine you are going to start a club for people of different cultures to build friendships.
What activities could you include that don't require much money?
Write a list and compare your ideas with other people.

_____   _____

_____   _____

_____   _____

Speaking activity 3 – Discuss your ideas

The "Some bubble-gum fun' story describes Justin and Honey's mother as 'an optimist when times get tough'. Discuss your idea about what that means.

Consonant clusters

There are 21 English consonants letters. They are:

b, c, d, f, g, h, j, k, l, m, n, p, q, r, s, t, v, w, x, y, z

This section provides practice with words with two or more consonants occurring together in words.
For example: The words <u>st</u>uff and <u>gr</u>uff have two consonants together at the *beginning* of the word.
The words you<u>ng</u> adu<u>lts</u> have consonants together at the *end* of the words.

Firstly, it is helpful to understand which combinations of letters and sounds are used in English.

- Draw a line through the letters that are <u>never</u> used together at the <u>beginning</u> of English words.
- Tick ✓ the consonants that <u>are used at the beginning</u> of English words.

k̶g̶   **sw** ✓   **tr**   **gr**   **br**   **st**   **fr**   **tg**   **cl**   **dm**   **kf**

Match the words *beginning* with a consonant cluster to a picture by writing the complete word.

sw

s̲w̲i̲n̲g̲   g r _ _ _ _   _ _ _ _   _ _ _ _ _   _ _ _ _   _ _ _ _ _   _ _ _ _

Find more words in the '**Some bubble-gum fun'** story with the same consonant clusters.
Write them on the lines below. Answers, page 83.

gr_____   st_____   cl_____   br_____   tr_____   fr_____

gr_____   st_____   cl_____   br_____

Practice with consonant clusters

How many words can you find in the puzzle below <u>beginning</u> with the letters **str, scr** or **spr**?
Circle or highlight the words appearing Across → and Down ↓

If necessary, use your dictionary to help by checking words beginning with 'scr', 'spr' and 'str'
and then checking which words are also in the puzzle below.

w	v	s	t	r	a	i	g	h	t	w	s	c	r	e	a	m	b
y	n	b	s	c	r	o	l	l	y	s	c	r	a	t	c	h	o
x	p	s	t	r	e	a	m	z	s	c	r	a	p	e	h	v	l
z	s	t	r	i	n	g	k	w	x	r	e	m	s	n	g	s	s
s	t	r	e	t	c	h	r	p	t	e	w	s	t	r	i	c	t
p	r	a	s	t	r	u	g	g	l	e	q	t	r	v	y	r	r
r	i	y	s	p	r	e	e	x	p	n	w	z	i	t	f	u	e
i	p	s	t	r	o	k	e	h	s	b	r	x	k	l	m	b	e
g	x	w	s	t	r	o	l	l	v	s	p	r	e	a	d	w	t
s	p	r	i	n	k	l	e	x	s	p	r	i	n	g	v	g	x
n	o	s	p	r	a	y	s	h	s	t	r	o	n	g	e	s	t

See answers, page 84.

Spelling lists – Words with the short vowel sound in 'b<u>u</u>bble g<u>u</u>m'

- Write words from the **'B<u>u</u>bble g<u>u</u>m'** story with the short vowel sound in the word **b<u>u</u>bble**. (There are more than 30 words)
- Put words in the correct column according to its spelling pattern. Then you can compare your list with the 'Spelling Reference Lists' at the back of the '**Rhyming Stories**' storybook.

u	o	ou
J<u>u</u>stin b<u>u</u>bble g<u>u</u>m	H<u>o</u>ney	y<u>ou</u>ng
–		

Write words for things illustrated on the b<u>u</u>bble picture page (p. 12) with the short sound in b<u>u</u>bble. There are more than 8 words.

u	o	ou
bubbles	brother	youngsters

Three ways of spelling the consonant sound /f/

There are three ways to spell the sound /f/. Look at the following words and underline the part that is pronounced as the sound /f/.

father   photo   tough

Practice

Use the clues below to write the correct word next to its meaning.
All the words contain the consonant sound /f/ but are written with 'f', 'ph' or 'gh'.

free ✓	feet	photograph	laughs	family	enough	physical
fun	graphics	elephant	phone	rough	pamphlet	

1. not costing any money   -   _____free_____

2. enjoyment or pleasure   -   _____

3. you use a camera to make one of these   -   _____

4. a person does this when something is funny   -   _____

5. the people who are related to you   -   _____

6. relating to the body   -   _____

7. people walk on these   -   _____

8. a very large animal with big ears and a long trunk (nose) -   _____

9. used to speak over long distances   -   _____

10. not smooth   -   _____

11. a very thin booklet that gives information   -   _____

12. images shown on a computer screen   -   _____

13. not too much and not too little but...   -   _____

Answers, page 84.

Add the words to each list below:

f	ph	gh
father	photocopy	tough

Rhyming Stories – Language activities for 'Connie's 'Orange Spot' coffee shop'

Words with the same vowel sound as in 'orange spot'

Write the words in the box next to their meaning, then write them in the crossword.

swap ✓	want	often	quality	doctors	block	wrong	shop	lots
	across	froth	non-stop	the lot	option		watch	

1. exchange something for something else - _____swap_____

2. on the opposite side - _____

3. describing something that is well made and of a good standard - _____

4. people with medical qualifications whose job is to treat sick patients - _____

5. a choice - _____

6. a small clock, usually worn on a person's wrist - _____

7. a large building with offices - _____

8. to hope to have or do something - _____

9. a place where you can buy things (noun); to buy things (verb) - _____

10. without stopping, continually happening - _____

11. everything that you need or want - _____

12. small white bubbles on the top of liquid - _____

13. not right or not correct - _____

14. many, a large number of people or things - _____

15. regularly, frequently - _____

Read and listen to the story about 'Connie's 'Orange Spot' coffee shop'.

Comprehension questions:

1. Where is Connie's coffee shop? _____

2. What can shoppers buy at Connie's shop?

_____

Listen to the rhyming story again.

Write in the missing words that have the same vowel sound as 'orange spot':

Connie has a coffee <u>shop</u>

where lots of people love to _____,

to sit and chat before they _____.

Her shop is called the 'Orange_____'.

across the road from a parking_____.

It's near a doctor's office _____

where patients visit 'round the_____.

It's painted orange, top to _____,

with tables cloths of orange _____.

She makes hot chocolate , sweet and _____

so many customers can't be _____ !

Her meals are always nice and _____

so doctors drop in quite a _____.

Fresh orange juice is served _____ _____

or hot, strong coffee, froth on_____.

There's orange cake, if it's not all_____.

Her 'goodies' list goes on and _____!

If quality gifts are what you _____

then Connie's shop has got the_____:

orange clocks and ladies _____,

coffee pots or chocolate _____.

Orange bottles, short or _____;

you can even swap if there's something _____.

Cash is fine and credit's an_____

You can see why people shop there _____!

Spelling and pronunciation practice

One word in each line <u>doesn't</u> have the same vowel sound as 'orange spot'? Circle the different word.

1.	shop	top	love	stop
2.	got	goes	wrong	want
3.	what	hot	short	long
4.	strong	so	box	pot

Speaking activity – ask three people the questions below and write short answers.

Survey questions	Name:	Name:	Name:
1. Do you drink coffee every day?			
2. Do you meet for coffee with friends often?			
3. What is your favourite place to shop?			
4. Do you like shopping for gifts?			
5. What's the most unusual gift you've ever received?			

Pronunciation of the consonant letter 's'

The letter 's' can be pronounced as the sound /s/ in <u>s</u>it and the sound /z/ in hi<u>s</u>.

Some guidelines for pronouncing 's'

- The letter 's' is always pronounced /s/ at the beginning of words (except as 'sh', e.g. <u>sh</u>op)
- When the letter 's' follows a vowel sound in a word, it is often pronounced as /z/.

Read the following clues for the words below and write them in the correct column. (Answers, page 85.)

Words pronounced with the sound /s/

1) opposite meaning to 'weak'
2) to exchange something
3) something you sing
4) opposite meaning to 'hard'
5) a small round mark
6) You do this when you see a red traffic light.

Words pronounced with the sound /z/

1) past word for is'
2) this means 'belonging to him'
3) this means 'belonging to her'
4) third person form of 'go'
5) third person form of 'do'
6) third person form of 'have'

Write the answers to the clues in the correct list below, depending on the pronunciation of the letter 's'.

Words with the letter 's' pronounced as sound /s/	Words with the letter 's' pronounced as sound /z/
1)	1)
2)	2)
3)	3)
4)	4)
5)	5)
6)	6)

Spelling lists – Words with the short vowel sound in '<u>o</u>range sp<u>o</u>t'

- Write words from story about '**Connie's shop**' with the short vowel sound in the words <u>o</u>range sp<u>o</u>t. (There are more than 30 words)
- Put words in the correct column according to its spelling pattern. Then you can compare your list with the 'Spelling Reference Lists' at the back of the '**Rhyming Stories**' storybook.

o	a
coffee	wh<u>a</u>t

Write words for things on the <u>orange</u> picture page (p. 14) with the short sound in <u>o</u>range sp<u>o</u>t.
There are more than 8 words.

o	a
coffee	watch

Rhyming Stories – Language practice for 'Charlie's marble carving'
Words with the same long vowel sound as in 'm**ar**ble c**ar**ving'

Write the words in the box next to their meaning, then write them in the crossword

art ✓	carve	marble	cart	market	half	large	calm
palms	target	park	craft	heart	smart	farm

1. very hard rock with a pattern of lines through it - _____

2. a place or event where people buy and sell - _____

3. the activity of painting, carving or making music etc. - _____art_____

4. an enclosed area of land with flowers, trees or play area - _____

5. clever, intelligent, thinking creatively - _____

6. carry or take something somewhere (with effort involved) - _____

7. trees with very long green leaves; they grow in warm places - _____

8. fifty percent - _____

9. land where vegetables, fruit or animals are produced as a business - _____

10. an activity needing skill; related to making things - _____

11. the shape and place representing love and strong feelings - _____

12. big - _____

13. peaceful, quiet and still - _____

14. the level or situation you want to achieve; a goal - _____

15. cut a design into the surface or make a shape from stone or marble - _____

Answers, page 86.

Read and listen to the story about 'Charlie's marble carving'.

Comprehension questions:

1. Where is Martin and Charlie's farm? _____

2. What do Martin and Charlie grow on their farm? _____

3. What does Charlie want to do more of in the future? _____

Listen to the rhyming story again.
Write in the missing words that have the same vowel sound as 'm<u>a</u>rble':

Charlie lives on a very large _____

where the days are hot but mainly _____.

He works very hard like many _____,

growing and picking bananas and <u>guavas</u>.

He also grows avocados and _____.

It's hard on his back and hard on his_____.

The farm belongs to his father, <u>Martin</u>

It's half an hour by car from _____.

Each week they cart fruit to the_____,

working hard to reach their_____.

But Charlie knows deep in his_____

all he really wants to do is_____.

He wants to make things out of_____;

artistic things for parks or a _____.

He loves designing the things he _____,

and never does any work by_____.

He often completes the work he _____

with beautiful patterns of stars or_____.

His father knows Charlie's skill for_____;

his work's spot-on and he's very_____.

*** ***

Martin's been to the bank for an overdraft

so Charlie can work full-time on his_____.

And little by little they'll decrease the_____

as Charlie expands his marble _____.

Spelling and pronunciation practice

One word in each line <u>doesn't</u> have the same vowel sound as 'ma<u>r</u>ble'? Circle the different word.

1.   farm   fruit   car   park
2.   hard   calm   can   carve
3.   all   palm   smart   art
4.   stars   heart   cart   back

Words with 'silent letters'

In English, many written words contain letters that are not pronounced. These letters are referred to as 'silent' letters. For example, the letter 'l' in 'calm' and 'palm' is not pronounced.

Read aloud the words in the box below and draw a line through the 'silent' letter in each word.
Check the words in your dictionary if you are unsure of the pronunciation or meaning.

foreign✓	half	often	listen	island	calf
column	palm	know	rhyme	hour	calm

Match each word in the box with its correct meaning in the list below.

1. from another country or another place   _____foreign_____
2. frequently   _____
3. sixty minutes   _____
4. have information in your mind   _____
5. fifty percent   _____
6. a strong, tall piece of stone or wood used to support a building   _____
7. a young cow   _____
8. land surrounded by water   _____
9. a tree with long green leaves; it grows well in warm places   _____
10. to hear and give attention when someone speaks   _____
11. peaceful, quiet and still   _____
12. words containing the same sounds   _____

Answers, page 87.

*Note: The word 'often' is usually pronounced with a silent 't', though some speakers pronounce the sound 't' in this word.

Spelling lists – Words with the long vowel sound in 'marble'

- Write words from **Charlie's** story with the long vowel sound in the word **ma̲r̲ble**.
  (There are more than 30 words)
- Put the word in the columns according to the spelling pattern. You can check the correct words in 'Spelling Reference Lists' at the back of the **Rhyming Stories** book.

ar	a	al
Charlie *farm*	*bana̲nas*	*calm*
Also: heart		

Write words for things illustrated on the **marble** picture page (p.16) with the long sound in **ma̲r̲ble**.
There are more than 8 words.

ar	a	al
ca̲rver	*bana̲nas*	*pa̲lms*

Rhyming Stories – Language activities for 'Nick's pink gym'
Words that have the vowel sound as in 'pink'

Write the words in the box next to their meaning, then write them in the crossword

rhythm✓	bistro	typical	quit	brilliant	picnic	wink	musician
slim	kick	building	gym	dish	pretty	thrill	vision

1. a regular pattern of music or sound   -   _____rhythm_____

2. having a healthy weight; to be thin, but not too thin   -   _____

3. making a structure from brick, wood or metal   -   _____

4. to quickly close and open one eye to show friendliness or approval   -   _____

5. a strong feeling of joy or pleasure   -   _____

6. a meal that you take with you to eat outside   -   _____

7. very skilled and clever   -   _____

8. to stop doing something   -   _____

9. a person who plays music   -   _____

10. to move something, such as a ball, with your foot   -   _____

11. attractive and pleasant to look at   -   _____

12. food that is prepared as part of a meal   -   _____

13. an informal restaurant   -   _____

14. an idea or mental picture of something that is possible   -   _____

15. a building with equipment for doing exercises   -   _____

16. the usual thing   -   _____

Answers, page 88.

Read and listen to the story about 'Nick's pink gym'.
Comprehension questions:

1. What was Nick's vision? _____

2. What are some things Kim pictured in Nick's gym? _____

Listen to the 'Nick's pink gym' rhyming story again.
Write in the missing words that have the same vowel sound as 'pink':

Nick had a vision to build a big _____

so he asked for some tips from designer friend _____.

Nick pictured it different; not a typical _____

so he asked her to draw up plans for_____.

Kim went to the site near the top of a _____

And sat there thinking, quiet and_____.

As Kim looked around, thinking where to _____,

she began to see where a gym would_____ _____.

A gym needs equipment to keep people_____

but it needs a lot more, if no-one's to _____.

A gym needs a pool so people can _____

and fun things to do, to help them stay_____.

Kim pictured a garden, somewhere pretty to_____,

where women would meet and chat for_____ _____.

She pictured a pond with a bridge and some _____

and a bistro that serves a good, healthy_____;

a place where children could play, run and _____

and families could sit and have a _____.

She pictured friends meeting together in_____

to swing to rhythms of musicians who_____.

Kim pictured the gym built up on the _____;

she pictured it finished and felt quite a _____.

She envisaged the building painted bright _____

but wasn't sure what her friend Nick would_____.

So she shared some ideas on the building with_____

and they both agreed he should start building _____.

Nick loved the idea of the gym being _____

'You're a brilliant designer!' said Nick with a _____!

Spelling and pronunciation practice

One word in each line __doesn't__ have the same vowel sound as 'pink'? Circle the different word.

1.	slim	sit	site	still
2.	quit	quite	quick	fit
3.	bridge	dish	fish	friend
4.	high	hill	build	thrill

(Answers, page 88.)

Speaking Activity 1 – Ask three people the questions below and write short answers.

Survey questions	Name:	Name:	Name:
1. Do you think gyms are a good idea?			
2. Have you ever used a gym ?			
3. Do you exercise every day?			
4. Do you think a gym needs more than exercise equipment to be useful to you?			
5. What is the name of a gym in your area?			

Speaking Activity 2

In groups of three or four, discuss the advantages and disadvantage of joining a gym to stay physically fit.
Then discuss the advantages and disadvantage of buying equipment to exercise at home.
Use the table below or draw a larger table like the one below to list ideas in each column:

Advantages of using a gym	Disadvantages of using a gym	Advantages of exercise at home	Disadvantages of exercise at home

After completing each list, what conclusion did your group reach about the advantages and disadvantages of gyms?

Speaking Activity 3

In groups of three or four, discuss the best layout for Nick's gym.
Use another piece of paper to draw a rough plan. Discuss what to include and where to put things.
Compare your ideas with people from other groups

Spelling lists – Words with the short vowel sound in 'p**i**nk g**y**m'

- Write words from the story about '**Nick's gym** with the short vowel sound in the word **pink**. (There are more than 30 words)
- Put the words in the columns according to the spelling pattern. You can check you have the correct words in 'Spelling Reference Lists' at the back of the '**Rhyming Stories'** storybook.

i	y	ui
Nick	*gym*	*b**ui**ld*
Also: *pr**e**tty w**o**men*		

Write words for things on the **'pink gym'** picture page (p. 18) with the short sound in p**i**nk.
There are more than 8 words.

i	y	ui
equipment	*gym*	*building*
Also: *pr**e**tty w**o**men*		

The consonant letter 'g' can be pronounced in different ways:

- The most common way to pronounce the letter 'g' is like the first sound in the words **'go'**, **'got'** and **'gap'**.

- 'g' can also be pronounced as the first sound the words **'gym'** and **'gentlemen'**. You can check the word **'gym'** in your dictionary to see the symbol your dictionary uses to represent this sound?

- 'g' can also be a 'silent letter'. This means it is not pronounced.

Read the following clues for words below. The answers all contain the letter 'g' (the 'g' sound isn't always at the beginning of the word). Write the answers below.

Words with the sound in 'go'	Words with the sound in 'gym'	'g' as a 'silent letter'
1) the opposite meaning to 'bad'	7) an indoor place for exercise	13) opposite meaning to 'dark'
2) to have the same idea	8) a precious stone	14) opposite meaning to 'wrong'
3) to get bigger	9) to be kind and careful	15) person who plans things
4) a big smile	10) have a picture in your mind	16) not low
5) the opposite meaning to 'stop'	11) you walk on this to go across a river	
6) a place with flowers and trees	12) not detailed or specific	

Write the answers to the clues in the correct list below, depending on the pronunciation of the letter 'g'.

Words with the letter 'g' pronounced as the first sound in 'go'	Words with the letter 'g' pronounced as the first sound in 'gym'	Words with 'g' as a 'silent letter'
1) good	7) gym	13) light
2)	8)	14)
3)	9)	15)
4)	10)	16)
5)	11)	
6)	12)	

Write words from above into the crossword.

Answers, page 89.

Guidelines for pronouncing 'g':

As explained on the previous page, the consonant letter 'g' can be pronounced in different ways.

Look at the word 'gorge' * which has two 'g's.

The first 'g' is pronoun like the sound in **go**; the second 'g' is pronounced like the sound in gym

* 'Gorge' means 'a deep, narrow valley cut through rock'.

If you check a dictionary that shows pronunciation, you will see a different sound symbol for each 'g' in 'gorge'.

Guidelines and practice:

The letter 'g' is always pronounced as the first letter in '**go**' when it comes before letters 'o', 'a' or 'u' or before another consonant sound; except when it is silent.

For example:

goat   **go**lf    **ga**te    **ga**rlic   **gu**m   **gu**n

Use a dictionary to find more words beginning with 'g' with the same spelling and pronunciation pattern:

go_____   go_____   ga_____   ga _____   gu_____   gu_____

The letter 'g' is always pronounced as the first letter in '**glad**' when it comes before another consonant sound:

glass   **gl**oves   **gr**ass   **gr**apes

Use a dictionary to find more words with the same spelling and pronunciation pattern:

gl_____   gl_____   gr_____   gr_____

'**g**' is generally silent when it comes before the letter 'h' or the letters 'th'

For example:

li**gh**t   ri**gh**t   len**gth** 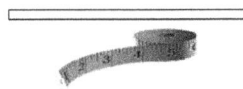   stren**gth**

The letter 'g' is generally pronounced like the sound in '**g**ym' when it comes before a final letter 'e' .
For example:

hin**ge**   pa**ge**    brid**ge**

However, there are exceptions so always check your dictionary when in doubt.

Rhyming Stories – Language activities for 'Good books about wood and cooking'
Words that have the vowel sound as in 'wood' and 'good'

Write the words in the box next to their meaning, then write them in the crossword

cushions	wool	could	wood	sugar	stood
good looking	shook	woman	pudding✓	cookies	should

1. a sweet, soft cooked dessert dish, made with rice, flour or bread -   _____pudding_____

2. a sweetener, obtained from a plant   -   _____

3. a word used to give advice   -   _____

4. an adult female   -   _____

5. the soft thick covering on sheep; the thick thread made from this -   _____

6. these are put on chairs to give more comfort   -   _____

7. sweet biscuits   -   _____

8. used with a verb to show what was or is possible -   _____

9. attractive   -   _____

10. past tense of the verb 'shake'   -   _____

11. this comes from trees and is used to make buildings -   _____

12. past tense verb of 'stand'   -   _____

Answers, page 90.

Read and listen to the story about 'Good books about wood and cooking'.
Comprehension questions:

1. What kind of books does Brook enjoy and sell? _____

2. How is Brook's friend, Anouk, described? _____

3. Why did Abdul phone the bookshop? _____

4. What happened when Abdul saw Anouk? _____

Listen to the 'Good books about wood and cooking' rhyming story again.
Write in the missing words that have the same vowel sound as 'wood':

Brook's a woman with a passion for_____,

and in her free time she gardens and _____.

She works in a bookshop so has time to _____

for popular fiction or the latest good _____.

The bookshop is spacious with walls made of _____.

She'd happily buy it, if only she _____.

The shop's always busy so her days are quite _____,

selling books about wood or knitting with _____.

People spend hours browsing and _____;

the most popular books being those about _____.

She works in the shop with her good friend <u>Anouk</u>

who's a good looking woman and a very good _____!

Her puddings and cookies all taste so _____,

she's written a cookbook, as Brook said she_____!

One day when the shop was particularly _____

a phone call came in from a man called _____.

He asked for a book called 'Cooking with_____',

said he wanted to buy it as soon as he _____.

Anouk took the order and had a good_____

but just couldn't find that particular_____.

'But we do have a cookbook that is very _____

I wrote it myself as my friend said I _____!'

He went to the bookshop to look for the _____

but couldn't stop staring when there stood _____!

His heart was racing and both his legs_____;

he would marry this woman, whatever it_____!

*** ***

Well, this story ends like a good romance _____

There's a wedding next June for Abdul and _____.

Spelling and pronunciation practice

One word in each line <u>doesn't</u> have the same vowel sound as 'wood'? Circle the different word.

1.	wool	work	wood	stood
2.	good	cook	could	call
3.	put	phone	took	look
4.	would	should	book	soon

Answers, page 90.

Speaking Activity 1

Ask people the following question to discover the most popular type of book.

What kind of books do you enjoy most?

✓ Put a tick next to the type of books that people say they enjoy:

Fiction (imagined stories & novels)	✓	Non-fiction (true stories, factual information)	✓
Romance stories		History books	
Adventure stories		Books on health and fitness	
Science-fiction stories		Cook books	
Crime stories		Biographies (true stories about people)	
Supernatural stories		Art books	
Funny stories		Gardening books	
		Craft books	
		Language books	

Speaking Activity 2 – Ask three people the questions below and write short answers.

Survey questions	Name:	Name:	Name:
1. Do you like browsing in bookshops?			
2. Do you prefer reading books or online?			
3. What is the latest book you've read?			
4. What is the best book you've ever read?			

Spelling lists – Words with the short vowel sound in 'g<u>oo</u>d w<u>oo</u>d'

- Write words from the story about **'Good books about wood and cooking'** with the short vowel sound in 'w<u>oo</u>d'. (There are more than 20 words)
- Put the words in the columns according to the spelling pattern. You can check you have the correct words in 'Spelling Reference Lists' at the back of the **'Rhyming Stories'** storybook (p. 84)

u	oo	ou
full	*Brook*	*could*
Also: w<u>o</u>man		

Write words for things on the **wood** picture page with the short sound in **wood**.
There are more than 8 words.

u	oo	ou
cushions	*cookbooks*	*Anouk*
Also: w<u>o</u>man		

Rhyming Stories – Language activities for 'Shirley's purple birthday'
Words that have the vowel sound as in 'p<u>ur</u>ple'
Write the words in the box next to their meaning, then write them in the crossword

purse ✓	surgeon	certain	fern	learns	nurse	hurt	encircle
	shirts	journal	worthwhile	versions	worse	swirls	

1. a small bag or case for carrying money   -   _____purse_____

2. to be useful and beneficial   -   _____

3. to be sure about something   -   _____

4. a doctor who is trained to perform medical operations   -   _____

5. a small book for regularly writing things that happen   -   _____

6. gets knowledge or skill in a new subject   -   _____

7. patterns of curved or circular lines   -   _____

8. more difficult or more unpleasant than before   -   _____

9. pieces of clothing for the top part of the body   -   _____

10. someone whose job is to care for sick or injured people   -   _____

11. a plant that has narrow leaves and no visible flowers   -   _____

12. to be in pain or injured   -   _____

13. to go around something, forming a circle around it   -   _____

14. different forms or varieties of something   -   _____

Answers, page 91.

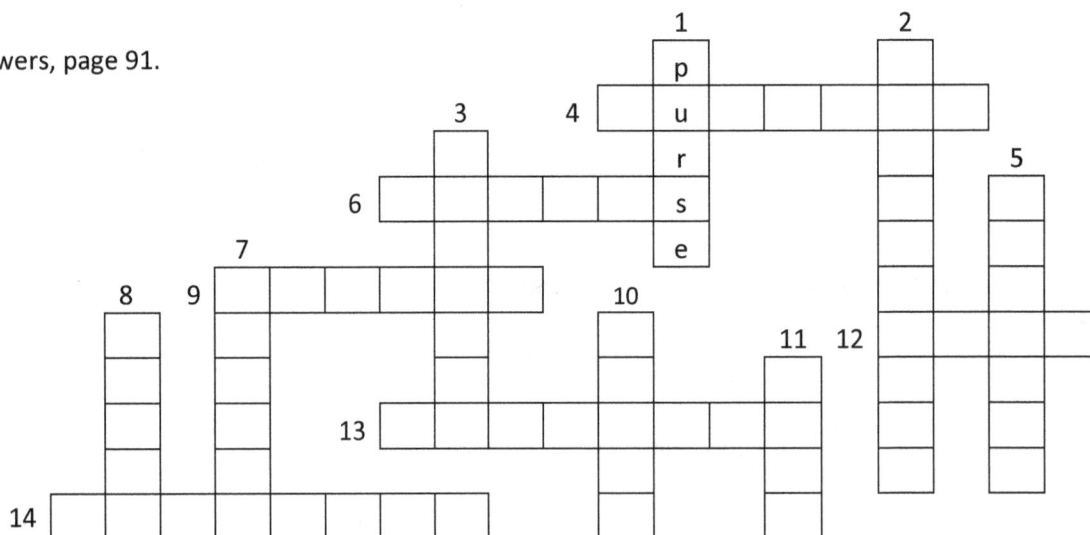

Read and listen to the story about 'Shirley's purple birthday'

Comprehension questions:

1. What does Shirley love about her work?_____

2. What purple things does Shirley have in her home?_____

3. What gifts did Shirley get for her birthday?_____

Listen to the 'Shirley's purple birthday' rhyming story again.
Write in the missing words that have the same vowel sound as 'purple':

Shirley lives and works in <u>Perth</u>.

It is the city of her _____.

She works as a nurse with a good friend _____,

attending patients, sick or _____.

As a nurse her main _____

are treating injury, breaks and _____.

When patients call she's always _____

to make certain that their pain's not _____.

She doesn't just work for the wage she _____;

but for all the worthwhile things she _____.

She loves observing busy _____

use medical skill in all its _____.

She's always kept a daily _____;

and like all her things, her journal's _____.

Her wardrobe's full of purple _____

that go with purple belts and _____.

And in her home you can be _____

that every room has a purple _____.

Last night she partied with the _____

in a brand new dress with purple _____.

Her boss said she should leave work_____;

it's not every day a girl turns_____!

Her girlfriends gave her a pretty_____,

a potted fern and purple _____;

and a lovely card with purple_____

encircled by some special _____:

'Happy Birthday', our girl _____!

You really, truly don't look _____!

The following story gives more details about the days before Shirley's birthday.
Complete the story about 'Shirley's Birthday Surprise' using words from the box.
All the words contain the same vowel sound as in 'pu_r_ple'

first	girl	heard	word	Thursday	
hurt	Bert	uncertain	curtain	thirty	Birthday

Soon it's Shirley's thirtieth birthday.

It's on the _ _ _ _ _ , which is next _ _ _ _ _ _ _ _ .

Her friends at work are in a _whirl_ (busy excitement)

making plans for the birthday _ _ _ _.

But of these plans Shirley hasn't _ _ _ _ _ ;

about her birthday, not one _ _ _ _ .

When Thursday arrived she felt quite _ _ _ _ _ ,

she hadn't even heard from _ _ _ _ .

She walked into work sad and _ _ _ _ _ _ _ _ _;

not seeing her friends hidden by the _ _ _ _ _ _ _ .

Then everyone called out 'Happy _ _ _ _ _ _ _ _ .'

and produced a cake with the number _ _ _ _ _ _ .!

Answers, page 91 – 92.

Spelling and pronunciation practice

One word in each line doesn't have the same vowel sound as 'pu_r_ple'? Circle the different word.

1. learn   heard   break   burn
2. whirl   girl   fern   friend
3. shirts   skirts   some   swirls
4. work   walk   word   nurse

Speaking activity – discuss the following questions

Have you ever been given or organised a 'surprise party'?

What do you usually like to do on your birthday?
Describe your idea of the perfect birthday celebration.

Imagine you are going to organise a surprise party for a friend.
Discuss your plans for the party.

Spelling lists – Words with the short vowel sound in 'pu<u>r</u>ple b<u>ir</u>thday'

- Write words from the story about '**Shi<u>r</u>ley's pu<u>r</u>ple b<u>ir</u>thday**' with the vowel sound in the words **pu<u>r</u>ple b<u>ir</u>thday**. (There are more than 30 words)
- Put the word in the columns according to the spelling pattern. You can check you have the correct words in 'Spelling Reference Lists' at the back of the **Rhyming Stories** book (p.85)

ir	er	or	ear	ur
birth	her	works	learns	nurse

Write words for things on the '**Shi<u>r</u>ley's pu<u>r</u>ple b<u>ir</u>thday**' picture page (p. 22) with the sound in **pu<u>r</u>ple**. There are more than 8 words.

ir	er	or	ur

Note: In some varieties of English (notably North American), the letter 'r' is pronounced when it follows a vowel sound. eg. th<u>ir</u>d, b<u>ir</u>d

The consonant letter 'c' can be pronounced two ways:

- 'c' can have the same pronunciation as /k/ in the words koala and kangaroo
  For example, the letter 'c' in cat, coat and clock have the same sound as /k/.

- 'c' can also be pronounced as the sound /s/
  For example, the letter 'c' in city, circle, certain have the same sound as /s/.
  At the end of a word, when 'c' is followed by a silent 'e' it sounds like /s/, as in peace and face.

Guidelines to pronouncing the letter 'c'

The letter 'c' is generally pronounced like the sound **'s '**when followed by the letters 'i', 'e' and 'y'.
The letter 'c' is generally pronounced as the sound **'k'** when followed by any other letter.

Note that often, in words with double 'c', such as accident, accept, accent, the first 'c' is pronounced like 'k', the second is pronounced like 's. Always check a dictionary if in doubt.

Write the words in the box next to its correct meaning below.
All words have the letter 'c' which is pronounced as /s/.

If you want to make this activity more challenging cover the words in the box and try to guess the correct words.

face	ice ✓	decided	niece	dance	mice	medicine
century	central	race	office	circle	cinema	nice
once	celebrate	rice	piece	December	city	

1. frozen water - _____ice_____

2. more than one mouse - _____

3. your brother's daughter - _____

4. this is taken by sick people to make you well - _____

5. to move your feet and body to music - _____

6. past verb form of 'decide' - _____

7. your eyes, nose and mouth are on this - _____

8. near or in the middle - _____

9. a competition of running to see who is fastest - _____

10. a hundred years - _____

11. a room where people work - _____

12. a round shape ◯ - _____

13. a building where people go to watch movies - _____

14. less than twice - _____

15. people do this on special days - _____

16. pleasant and good - _____

17. a popular food in Asia - _____

18. a part of something such as cake or cheese - _____

19. the last month of the year (Use a capital letter.) - _____

20. a very large town - _____

Write words from the previous exercise into the crossword.

Answers, page 91 – 92.

Rhyming Stories – 'Green fields, clean beaches'
Words that have the vowel sound as in 'gr<u>ee</u>n f<u>ie</u>lds'
Write the words in the box next to their meaning, then write them in the crossword

Greece	least✓	niece	believe	agree	peak	features	scenic
east	cheese	skied	pleased	sweet	steep	keen on	reasons

1. the smallest amount or minimum — _____least_____

2. a food that is made from milk; it can be soft or hard — _____

3. happy about a situation — _____

4. to think that something is true — _____

5. a country in southern Europe — _____

6. important qualities or parts of something — _____

7. the explanation or facts about why something is true — _____

8. the top of a mountain — _____

9. the daughter of your brother or sister — _____

10. to have the same opinion as someone — _____

11. describing the side of a mountain with a sharp upward angle — _____

12. opposite direction of 'west' — _____

13. travelled over snow with special equipment on your feet — _____

14. describing a naturally beautiful scene or place — _____

15. very interested in something or someone — _____

16. describing a kind, attractive person — _____

Answers, page 93.

[Crossword grid with numbered clues 1-16; vertical word "l e a s t" spelled at position 1]

Comprehension questions:

1. What has Gina seen in New Zealand? _____

2. Why did Steve keep eating cheese and drinking tea? _____

3. Why do Dino and Nina believe they'll be seeing Gina in future seasons?_____

Listen to the 'Green fields, clean beaches' rhyming story again.
Write in the missing words with the same vowel sound as 'green':

Dino and Nina come from _____

but now they live much further _____.

They're in New Zealand where it's very _____.

You're sure to agree, if you've ever _____.

Three weeks ago, their youngest _____

came to see them, all the way from_____.

Her name is Gina; she's twenty _____.

She's gentle and sweet, they both _____.

So far she's seen a lot of _____

and climbed some mountains, very _____.

Of all New Zealand's scenic _____

she loves the quiet, clean, peaceful _____.

When Dino's friend, a young man, _____

came to visit, he wouldn't _____.

He ate more cheese and drank more _____

as Gina described what she planned to _____.

Steve asked her if she'd ever _____.

She hadn't, so they soon _____

to drive up to a mountain _____

and have a ski the following _____.

As Dino and Nina watched their _____

they were very pleased, to say the _____.

They really believe, for very good _____

they'll be seeing their niece in future_____.

She seems to be so keen on _____,

they're hoping that she'll never _____.

Spelling and pronunciation practice

One word in each line doesn't have the same vowel sound as 'green'? Circle the different word.

1.	niece	nice	east	least
2.	clean	their	green	tea
3.	three	cheese	week	were
4.	beach	leave	ski	climb

Answers, page 93.

Spelling guidelines

The most usual way to spell words with the same vowel sound as in gr<u>ee</u>n is with 'ee' but there are other spelling variations, as you can see in the 'Green fields, clean beaches' story and in the columns on the opposite page.

Some words with the long vowel sound as in 'green' are spelt with ' ie' (e.g. n<u>ie</u>ce)
but a few words are spelt with 'ei'

A spelling rule to remember for this sound is:

Use 'i' before 'e', except after 'c';
(After the letter 'c', we write 'ei')

Example words with 'i' before 'e' are: n<u>ie</u>ce   bel<u>ie</u>ve   rel<u>ie</u>ve   sk<u>ie</u>d

Example words with 'ei' after the letter 'c' are: rec<u>ei</u>ve   rec<u>ei</u>pt

More examples of ' ie' spelling:

Complete the following words with 'ie'

Answers, page 94

p _ _ce   f_ _ lds   sh _ _ld   th _ _ f

Speaking Activity
Ask three people questions below and write short answers.

Survey questions Names			
1. Have you been to Greece?			
2. Have you been to New Zealand?			
3. Have you ever skied on steep peaks?			
4. What country or area is the greenest place you have ever seen?			

Research Activity

Research the scenic features of a particular country.
Choose any country you would like to visit.

What natural scenic features can tourists see?

What man-made features can tourists see?

Tell your group about the information you learnt from your research.

Spelling lists – Words with the long vowel sound in 'gr<u>ee</u>n f<u>ie</u>lds'

- Write words from the story about '**Gr<u>ee</u>n f<u>ie</u>lds, cl<u>ea</u>n beaches**' with the long vowel sound in '**gr<u>ee</u>n**'. (There are more than 30 words)
- Put the words in the columns according to the spelling pattern. You can check you have the correct words in 'Spelling Reference Lists' at the back of the **Rhyming Stories** book (p.86).

ea	ee	ie	e	i
east	*Greece*	*niece*	*Steve*	*ski*

Write words for things on the **green** picture page (p. 24) with the short sound in **green**.
There are more than 8 words.

ea	ee	ie	e	i
features	*green*	*niece*	*Steve*	*Gina*
Also: people				

Spelling and pronunciation - homophones

Some English words are pronounced exactly the same way as another word, but it has a different meaning and/or spelling. These words are called **homophones** (meaning 'same sound'). For example, 'week' which means 'seven days' and 'weak' which means 'not strong', have the same pronunciation.

Put the words '**week**' and '**weak**' in the correct place in the following sentence:

She is still feeling _____ after a _____ in bed with the flu.

Further practice

Choose the appropriate word (from the choice given for each sentence) and complete the sentences. Use your dictionary if necessary.

peace/piece

1) I won't have any _____ until I find the last _____ of the puzzle.

meat/meet

2) I'll _____ you outside the supermarket after I buy the _____ for dinner.

reel/real

3) The young boy wants a _____ fishing line and _____ this year, in place of the fishing net he used last year

seen/scene

4) The accident _____ was the most terrible thing I have ever _____.

steel/steal

5) The _____ bars were so heavy, nobody could _____ them.

leased/least

6) We _____ the office for a year because it was the _____ expensive way to start our business.

sea/see

7) You can _____ all the way to the _____ from here.

been/bean

8) I've _____ making _____ soup while you've _____ sleeping.

peek/peak

9) 'When I reach the mountain _____ I'll _____ over the top.'

Answers, page 94.

Consonant sounds at the end of words

Some languages don't contain words with a final consonant sound, so when learning English, these words can cause difficulty for those learners of English.

The following example words demonstrate how a final consonant completely changes the meaning of a word.

Say the following words from left to right to practise words with and without a final consonant:

words without a final consonant:		words with a final consonant:
she	⟶	sheep
me		meet
pea		peak
we		week
knee		niece
see		scene
be		been
key		keen

More words with the long vowel sound in 'gr<u>ee</u>n'

Think of English words for things in the following categories.
See how many words you can think of in each category in three minutes.
All the words must contain the long vowel sound in 'gr<u>ee</u>n' and the words must be English.

Thing to eat

Places to go

Animals to see

See page 94 to check your answers.

Rhyming Stories – Language activities for 'Paul's cork boards'

Words that have the same vowel sound as in 'c<u>or</u>k b<u>oar</u>ds'

Write the words in the box next to their meaning, then write them in the crossword

bought	install	reporter	order	boards	quarter ✓	thought
rewarding	cork	store	awful	war	for sure	
corner	boring	borders				

1. 25% (twenty-five per cent)   -   _____quarter_____
2. put something new somewhere and make it ready for use   -   _____
3. past verb form of 'think'   -   _____
4. flat pieces of wood, cork or plastic   -   _____
5. put in a request for something you want to buy   -   _____
6. past verb form of 'buy'   -   _____
7. it is certain, without any doubt   -   _____
8. someone whose job is to report information and events   -   _____
9. bad and unpleasant   -   _____
10. the place where two walls meet together   -   _____
11. making you feel satisfied and happy with what you've done   -   _____
12. light soft material obtained from a particular tree   -   _____
13. fighting between groups of people   -   _____
14. a shop or warehouse where goods are sold to the public   -   _____
15. not interesting   -   _____
16. the lines around the edge of something   -   _____

Answers, page 95.

Read and listen to the story about 'Paul's cork boards'.

Comprehension questions:

1. What was Paul's job before and why was it awful? _____

2. What did Paul and Dawn put in the sports store? _____

Listen to the rhyming story about 'Paul's cork boards' again.
Write in the missing words that have the same vowel sound as 'cork':

Paul was a TV news reporter

who travelled the country from border to _____

sometimes reporting the good things he _____

but mostly reporting on trouble and _____.

One day he'd driven an hour and a _____

when he had a call from his eldest _____:

'Hey Dad. You said your job's awful and _____

and that you need something more _____!

Remember the sports store, the one on the_____?

They've reduced its price by more than a_____!'

Paul thought a lot about buying the _____

then called his wife Dawn to talk some_____.

They'd never run a store _____

but Dawn said, 'What're we waiting_____!'

So they bought the store and installed new_____.

They put cork on the walls and cork on the _____.

They filled the store with T-shirts and_____

and ordered balls for all sorts of _____.

The store sold things for field, court and _____

and soon they needed help from their_____.

Dawn thought they needed cork boards for the_____

so they ordered forty; some short and some _____.

They ordered boards with all sorts of _____

and soon, they couldn't keep up with the_____!

Paul often works from four in the _____

but one things for sure, his life isn't _____!

Spelling and pronunciation practice

One word in each line doesn't have the same vowel sound as 'cork'? Circle the different word.

1.	short	store	work	more
2.	call	war	wall	are
3.	board	good	door	floor
4.	saw	for	sure	new

Answers, page 95.

Spelling lists – Words with the long vowel sound in 'cork boards'

- Write words from story about '**Cork boards,**' with the vowel sound in '**c<u>or</u>k**'.
  (There are more than 30 words)
- Put the words in the columns according to the spelling pattern. You can check you have the
  correct words in 'Spelling Reference Lists' at the back of the **Rhyming Stories** book (p. 87).

or oor	ou	a	ar	aw
reporter door	*thought*	*call*	*war*	*saw*
Also: Paul				

Write words for things on the **cork** picture page (p. 26) with the sound in '**c<u>or</u>k**'.
There are more than 8 words.

or oor	ou	a	ar	aw
Also: oars				

Spelling and pronunciation - homophones

Some pairs of English words have the same pronunciation but different meanings and spelling patterns.

For example, '**bored**' which means 'uninterested' and '**board**' which means 'a flat piece of wood or cork, have the same pronunciation. These words are called homophones.

Put the words '**bored**' and '**board**' in the correct place in the following sentence:

He was _____ when he worked in the factory making _____.

Further practice

Choose the appropriate word (from the choice given for each sentence) and complete the sentences. Use your dictionary if necessary.

border/boarder

1. As a child I was a _____ at a boarding school near the northern _____ of the country.

course/coarse

2. They're fixing the uneven, _____ surface of the race _____ to make it safer for horses.

fore/four

3. Environmental issues are at the _____front and will stay that way for the next _____ decades.

morning/mourning

4. She's _____the loss of her little dog which died yesterday_____.

oar/or

5. 'Hold on to the _____tightly, _____ it will be difficult getting back to the shore.'

paw/pour

6. You should _____ some warm water over the poor injured cat's sore _____.

raw/roar

7. The lions will _____ loudly until the zookeeper gives them some _____ meat.

sure/shore

8. They're _____ they saw a large crocodile on the _____ of the bay.

saw/sore

9. When I _____the accident victim, I knew he'd be _____ for a long time.

war/wore

10. The band _____ uniforms when they marched to the _____ memorial.

you're/your

11. 'If you don't do _____ homework _____ going to fail the exam! '

Answers, page 96.

Rhyming Stories – Language activities for 'Prue's blue music school'
Words that have the same vowel sound as in 'bl<u>ue</u> sch<u>oo</u>l'

Write the words in the box next to their meaning, then write them in the crossword

view	refuse ✓	huge	beauty	school	group
lose	choose	no clue	confused	tutor	through
pursuit	studio	cool	youth	noodles	

1. say you will not accept something — _____refuse_____

2. to have no ideas, not know or understand — _____

3. school where students learn to give beauty treatments — _____

4. very large — _____

5. a plan or activity that a person follows for a period of time — _____

6. a teacher who teaches a student or a small group — _____

7. unable to think clearly about something — _____

8. some people together — _____

9. an expression that can mean 'wonderful, good, great' — _____

10. young people — _____

11. a room used for music, art or photography — _____

12. to decide and select which things you want — _____

13. to not have something because it's gone or lost — _____

14. from the beginning of something to the end — _____

15. the things you can see — _____

16. long pieces of pasta made from flour, egg and water — _____

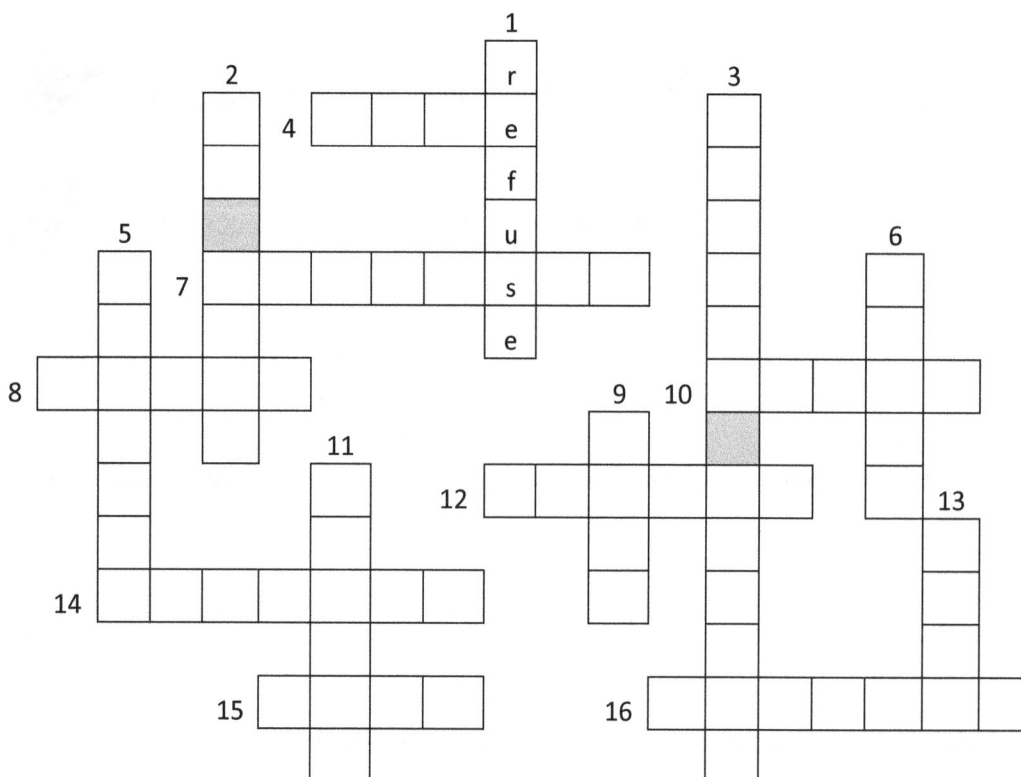

Answers, page 97.

Read and listen to the story about 'Prue's blue music school'
Comprehension questions:

1. List the types of work that Prue had tried: _____ _____

_____ _____ _____

2. What does she really love doing? _____

3. What did she decide to start and what will she call it? _____

Listen to the 'rhyming story 'Prue's blue music school' again.
Write in the missing words that have the same vowel sound as 'blue':

Prue sat at her desk, staring out at the _____

considering her future and what she could_____.

She was still in her youth; only twenty _____,

but as jobs go, she'd had quite a_____.

She'd worked a few months in a new beauty_____

and taught kids to swim in a huge outdoor_____.

She'd worked in a shop selling noodles and_____

and tutored young students in a school music_____.

She'd worked in a store selling boots and _____

but she still had no clue what career path to_____.

Friends offered advice which she usually_____;

hearing all their ideas just made her _____!

Then she met for a chat with her good friend _____

who listened as Prue began talking things _____.

'I love playing music, especially the _____;

I could make music my career _____.

But I don't think I'd like to teach music in _____.

The groups are too big; there're too many _____.'

Then suddenly the truth became clear to Prue:

to improve her future, she knew what to_____!

'I'm going to start my own music _____;

something fun and new and modern and _____.

Somewhere roomy and bright - all painted in _____.

I'll promote it on YouTube and for students to _____.'

'I'll open in June; there's no time to_____!

Now I can't wait to spread the good_____.

I'll call the school 'Prue's Studio_____'.

I'm so happy now I know what to _____!'

Spelling and pronunciation practice

One word in each line <u>doesn't</u> have the same vowel sound as 'bl<u>ue</u>'?

Circle the different word.

1.	good	school	pool	too
2.	soup	group	young	youth
3.	true	blue	fun	flute
4.	could	through	view	knew

Spelling and pronunciation - homophones

Some pairs of English words have the same pronunciation but different meanings and spelling patterns.

For example, '**blue**' means 'the colour of the sky' and '**blew**' is the past verb of 'blow'.
Words that have the same pronunciation are called 'homophones'.

Put the words '**blue**' and '**blew**' in the correct place in the following sentence:

The leaves_____ off the tree in the strong wind and fell into the _____ water.

Further practice

Choose the appropriate word (from the choice given for each sentence) and complete the sentences. Use your dictionary if necessary.

flew/flu

1. My husband had the _____ last week but he still _____ to New York.

new/knew

2. As soon as the woman saw the _____ car, they _____ her husband would buy it.

queue/cue

3. When the movie producer gave the _____, the actors stood in the_____.

two/too/to

4. This is _____ heavy for _____ people to carry; we need more people _____ help us.

through/threw

5. The boy _____ the ball _____ the gate and into the park.

Answers, page 97.

Speaking activity

Discuss the following topic in small groups:

How many different jobs have you had during your life?

Talk about the best and worst job you have ever had.

 © Boyer Educational Resources

Spelling lists – Words with the long vowel sound in 'Prue's blue music school'

- Write words from the story about **'Prue's blue school,'** with the vowel sound in 'blue'. (There are more than 30 words)
- Put the words in the columns according to the spelling pattern. You can check you have the correct words in 'Spelling Reference Lists' at the back of the **Rhyming Stories** book (p. 88).

oo	u (also ue)	o	ou	ew
school	Prue	do	soup	view

Write words for things on the **blue** picture page with the sound in '**blue**' (p. 28).
There are more than 8 words.

oo	u (also ue)	o	ou	ew

Rhyming Stories – Language activities for 'Howard Brown's mountain house'
Words that have the same vowel sound as 'br<u>ow</u>n h<u>ou</u>se'

Write the words in the box next to their meaning, then write them in the crossword.

house	found	clown around	frown	fountain	grounds
	run-down	no doubt	brown	proud ✓	
town	council	shower	crowds	tower	power

1. feeling very pleased with something you have done   -   _____proud_____

2. there is certainty, the situation is certain, definite   -   _____

3. do funny things to make people laugh; to act like a clown   -   _____

4. large groups of people   -   _____

5. past verb form of 'find'   -   _____

6. the organisation that makes decisions for a town   -   _____

7. the land around a particular organisation or building   -   _____

8. place in a bathroom where you wash by standing under a water spray   -   _____

9. tall, narrow structure or building, taller than other buildings in the area   -   _____

10. a place where people live   -   _____

11. a structure in a garden or park that makes water go into the air   -   _____

12. the colour of chocolate   -   _____

13. the look on a person's face when they are unhappy or worried   -   _____

14. a place where people live, work and shop   -   _____

15. energy such as electricity that provides light and heat to buildings   -   _____

16. old and in a bad condition, something that needs repairing   -   _____

Answers, page 98.

Read and listen to 'Howard Brown's mountain house'
Comprehension questions:

1. What is Howard's job? _____

2. Why did Howard move out of town and what did he buy? _____

_____

3. What improvements did Howard make? _____

Listen to the rhyming story again.
Write in the missing words that have the same vowel sound as in 'br<u>ow</u>n':

Howard Brown repairs old <u>houses</u>;

it's dirty work so he wears brown _____.

He also works 'round local _____

maintaining the parks and public_____.

He works for the council trimming _____

and digs out weeds for hours and_____.

He builds stone walls and puts in _____

around the town, near the southern_____.

Howard loves his work, there isn't a_____

as he sings aloud, working out and _____.

He's a happy man, never seems to _____;

he loves to joke and _____ _____.

But as more crowds moved into _____:

'It's time to move out,' thought Howard_____.

So he went to the mountains to look at _____

that he could improve with repairs and_____.

He found an old house that was very_____ - _____

which he bought; then thought about pulling it _____.

The house had no toilet, laundry or_____;

no gas or tower to provide him with _____.

But he got to work and very soon_____

the place was improving all_____.

He moved all rubbish from around the _____

and painted outside different shades of_____.

He put in flowers and built a <u>fountain</u>

and found he loved living up on the _____.

Now the grounds look great; it's all worked _____.

Howard's proud of his house – there's not a _____!

Spelling and pronunciation practice

One word in each line **doesn't** have the same vowel sound as 'br<u>ow</u>n'? (Circle the different word.

1.	doubt	down	brown	work
2.	crowd	loud	could	ground
3.	town	house	frown	bought
4.	four	out	proud	found

Words with 'silent letters'

In English, many written words contain letters that are not pronounced. These letters are called 'silent' letters. For example, the letter 'b' in 'doubt' is not pronounced.

- Read aloud the words in the box below and draw a light line through the 'silent' letter in each word.
- Write each word next to its meaning below.
- Check the words in your dictionary if you are unsure of the pronunciation or meaning.

climb	know	wrong	thumb	comb	plumber
knew	doubt	knock	write	debt	wrinkle	knee

1. to move upward   _climb_

2. to have information   _____

3. to put letters on paper   _____

4. something for your hair   _____

5. a job fixing water pipes   _____

6. not right   _____

7. not certain   _____

8. hit something to make a noise   _____

9. past verb for 'know'   _____

10. short finger on side of hand   _____

11. part of your leg   _____

12. something owed to someone   _____

13. a small line or fold of the skin   _____

Write the words next to the corresponding numbers in the crossword:

Answers, page 99.

There are some patterns with the use of silent consonants. Can you see which letters can go together?

Complete the information about silent consonants and write some more examples on the lines below:

Silent 'b' can **follow**   _m_   _cli**mb**_ _____

Silent 'b' can also **go before**   _t_   _____

At the **beginning** of words, silent 'k' can go before   _____   _____

At the **beginning** of words, silent 'w' can go before   _____   _____

Answers, page 99 - Also, see page 105 for lists of words with silent letters.

Spelling lists – Words with the vowel sound in 'br<u>ow</u>n h<u>ou</u>se'

- Write words from the story about **'Howard Brown's mountain house'** with the vowel sound in **'brown'**. (There are more than 20 words)
- Put the words in the columns according to the spelling patterns. You can check you have the correct words in 'Spelling Reference Lists' at the back of the **Rhyming Stories** book (p. 89).

ow	ou
Howard Br<u>ow</u>n	*grounds*

Write words for things on the **'Howard's br<u>ow</u>n h<u>ou</u>se'** picture page (p. 30) with the vowel sound in **br<u>ow</u>n**. There are more than 5 words.

ow	ou
run-d<u>ow</u>n	*house*

Rhyming Stories – Language activities for 'Grey day at the bay'
Words that have the same vowel sound as 'grey day' (see p. 62 for a note on spelling 'grey')

Write the words in the box next to their meaning, then write them in the crossword

complain	landscape	a break ✓	lake	cave	waves	sailing
waiting	games	eight	grey	bay	great	painting

1. a vacation or period of time away from work or school - _____ a break _____

2. say that something is wrong and you are upset about it - _____

3. staying in a place until something happens or someone arrives - _____

4. lines of water moving on the ocean's surface and on to the beach - _____

5. an area of natural countryside - _____

6. one more than seven - _____

7. a hole in the side of a mountain or under the ground - _____

8. an area of water with land all around it - _____

9. activities, entertainment or sport played for fun or competition - _____

10. the colour between black and white - _____

11. very good, important or famous - _____

12. a sport using boats with sails on the water - _____

13. to make pictures of places or things using paint and brushes - _____

14. a place where the sea is surrounded on three sides by land - _____

Answers, page 100.

Read and listen to 'Grey day at the bay'
Comprehension questions:

1. What plans did James and Kay make in May?_____

2. What was the weather like at Sandy Bay?_____

3. What indoor activity did Kay try? _____

4. What happened when Kay went back home?_____

Listen to the rhyming story again.

Write in the missing words that have the same vowel sound as 'gr<u>e</u>y':

James and Kay work hard every _____

and don't often take a_____.

But last year, at the end of _____,

they made some plans to go_____.

They'd planned to take an eight day_____

to a sunny place near a beach and a _____.

They'd planned to swim and surf the _____

and if they had time, maybe see some _____.

But when they arrived in 'Sandy_____'

the weather was cold and windy and _____.

'That's Okay' said James and _____.

'The weather won't spoil our _____!'

They went for a drive around the _____

and ordered coffee and chocolate _____.

They looked out the window, across the _____

and talked about swimming and sailing next _____.

But the weather forecast said there'd be more _____.

'Oh well', said James, 'We can't_____

There're indoor games while we're_____

or a course to take in landscape _____'

Well, as soon as Kay began to _____

the teacher knew that she'd be _____.

Back at home, eight months _____

Kay's become a famous_____!

And all because one rainy _____

she'd begun to paint at Sandy_____.

Her favourite painting to this _____

is of cold grey waves in a cold grey_____.

Spelling and pronunciation practice

One word in each line <u>doesn't</u> have the same vowel sound as 'grey'? Circle the different word.

1.	great	break	beach	grey
2.	cave	lake	wave	when
3.	they	take	eight	end
4.	paint	sail	said	rain

Answers, page 100.

Spelling lists – Words with the vowel sound in 'grey'

- Read through the '**Gr<u>e</u>y day at the B<u>ay</u>,**' story again.
- Find all the words with the same vowel sound in '**grey**'. (There are more than 20 words.)
- Write the words that you find in the story with the vowel sound in '**grey**' in the columns below.
- Put the words in the columns according to the spelling pattern.
  You can check you have the correct words in the correct column by checking 'Spelling Reference Lists' at the back of the **Rhyming Stories** book (p. 90).

ay	a	a + silent e	ai
Kay		James	sailing

Also: break, grey, eight

Note: The word 'grey' is written as 'gray' in North American English.

Write words for things illustrated on the gr<u>e</u>y picture page (p. 32) with the vowel sound in gr<u>e</u>y.
There are more than 8 words.

ay	a + silent e	ai

Also: break, grey

Spelling and pronunciation - homophones

Some pairs of English words have the same pronunciation but different meanings and spelling patterns.

For example, the word 'eight' represents a number and 'ate' is the past verb form of 'eat'. These words have the same pronunciation.

Put the words 'eight' and 'ate' in the correct place in the following sentence:

There were _____ small cakes on the plate but the boys _____ them all.

Further practice

Choose the appropriate word (from the choice given for each sentence) and complete the sentences. Use your dictionary if necessary.

brake /break

1) Did you _____ the glass in your car _____ lights when you had the accident?

grate/great

2) My friend gave me a _____ gift for my kitchen. I use it to _____ cheese and vegetables.

pain/pane

3) When the window _____ broke, I cut my hand. The _____ was very bad.

plain/plane

4) The _____ I arrived in was a _____ grey colour; the seats inside were plain grey too.

sail/sale

5) The ship with the big _____ has been for _____ for eight months and I want to buy it.

tail/tale

6) Have you heard the _____ called 'How the kangaroo got its_____'?

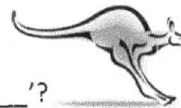

wait/weight
7) You should _____ till you lose more _____ before going in the race.

waste/waist

8) I don't want to _____ this food but I want to keep a slim _____ so I must stop eating.

way/weigh

9) The best _____ to _____ yourself is to do it the same time each day.

Answers, page 100.

Rhyming Stories – Language activities for 'Golden roses, yellow boats'

Words that have the same vowel sound as 'G<u>o</u>lden yell<u>ow</u> r<u>o</u>se'

Write the words in the box next to their meaning, then write them in the crossword.

on the whole	rowing	goal ✓	notion	joke
	won't	take over	global	
promote	golden	doze	coast	

1. a target, something to aim towards   -   <u>   goal   </u>

2. idea or opinion   -   _____

3. a short funny story told to make people laugh   -   _____

4. moving through the water using oars   -   _____

5. the colour of gold; also a colour similar to yellow   -   _____

6. international, worldwide   -   _____

7. take possession or management of something   -   _____

8. a short light sleep   -   _____

9. land along the shore; where land and ocean meet   -   _____

10. the shortened form of 'will not'   -   _____

11. an expression meaning something 'is generally true'   -   _____

12. to make more known or increase sales   -   _____

Answers, page 101.

Read and listen to the story about 'Golden roses, yellow boats'

Comprehension questions:

1. What is Joe's business? _____

2. What happened to Joe a month ago? _____

3. What are Flo and Joe planning now? _____

Listen to the rhyming story again.

Write in the missing words that have the same vowel sound as 'golden rose':

This is a photo of Flo and <u>Joe</u>

who came from Poland long _____.

As most of their friends and family _____

they don't miss the cold, or the _____.

Years ago they had the _____

of living near the Pacific _____.

Now their home is on the _____

with a business that they're proud of _____.

Their business has been slowly _____

Selling and renting boats for_____.

Noah, their son, helps with the _____.

He'll take over soon – or so Joe _____!

A month ago, on the coastal _____

Joe fell off his bike with a heavy _____.

He hurt his nose; his shin bone _____

but he tells the story as if it's a _____.

So although Joe loves his boats on the_____,

slowing down is now his _____.

Most of the day he reads or_____

while Flo spends time growing golden _____.

As Noah takes over, he won't be _____,

Joe can still take calls about boats on the _____.

And a door often opens as the past one _____;

Joe's going to promote Flo's golden_____.

The couple both know the roses she _____

could win first prize at global _____.

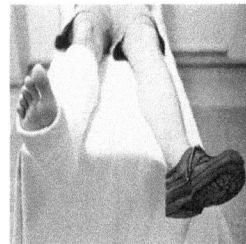

Spelling and pronunciation practice

One word in each line <u>doesn't</u> have the same vowel sound as 'g<u>o</u>ld'? (Circle) the different word.

1.	know	one	snow	row
2.	hopes	home	long	phone
3.	coast	boat	cold	month
4.	road	rose	most	son

Answers, page 101.

Spelling lists – Words with the vowel sound in 'G<u>o</u>lden r<u>o</u>se, yell<u>ow</u> b<u>oa</u>t'

- Write words from **Joe and Flo's** story in the correct columns below.
  (There are more than 30 words)
- Put the word in the columns according to the spelling pattern. You can check the correct words in 'Spelling Reference Lists' at the back of the **'Rhyming Stories'** storybook (p. 91)

o	o + silent 'e'	ow	oa
photo	Joe	know	coast

Also: although

Write words for things illustrated on the **'Golden roses, yellow boats'** picture page (page 34 of 'Rhyming Stories' storybook) with the vowel sound in **'g<u>o</u>lden r<u>o</u>ses'**. There are more than 10 words.

o	o + silent 'e'	ow	oa

Spelling and pronunciation - homophones

Some pairs of English words have the same pronunciation but different meanings and spelling patterns. For example, 'no' which means 'not any' and 'know' which means 'have information' have the same pronunciation. Words with the same pronunciation are called homophones.

Put the words '**no**' and '**know**' in the correct place in the following sentence:

There are _____ students in this class who _____the correct answer.

Further practice

Choose the appropriate word (from the choice given for each sentence) and complete the sentences. Use your dictionary if necessary. You can check you answers at the back of this book

1. rose/rows

Of all the flowers planted in _____, I think the _____ looks best.

2. a loan/alone

If you apply for __ _____from the bank, then you _____ should pay it back.

3. grown/groan

The jungle had _____ so thick that it was very difficult to find our way.

Even the experienced walkers began to _____with the struggle.

4. mown/moan

I always _____ a lot when the grass has to be _____.

5. so/sew(s)/sow(s)

The farmer and his wife work _____ well together.

He _____the seed while she_____ their clothes.

6. tows/toes

When he _____the old car through the gateway, stand well back or watch your _____.

7. whole/hole

At the construction site, I spent the _____ day digging a very large _____ !

8. road/rowed/rode

The boys _____their boats along the river,

while the girls _____their bikes along the _____.

Answers, page 101.

Rhyming Stories – Language practice for 'Choy's foil toys'
Words with the same vowel sound as in 'foil toys'

Write the words in the box next to their meaning, then write them in the crossword

toil	Hanoi ✓	lawyer	coil	foil	boisterous
noise	joys	soy	oil	soil	employer

1. bean of an Asian plant that is used as food and produced as sauce - _____

2. Capital city of Vietnam - __Hanoi____

3. pleasure, situations or activities that make you happy - _____

4. someone who employs other people to work for them - _____

5. a person whose job is to give advice about the law - _____

6. a sound, especially one that is loud or causes disturbance - _____

7. the ground in which plants grow - _____

8. excited and lively - _____

9. a fatty liquid, thicker than water and used for cooking - _____

10. a long thin piece of something bent into several circular bends - _____

11. metal made into very thin sheets for various uses - _____

12. work hard - _____

Answers, page 102.

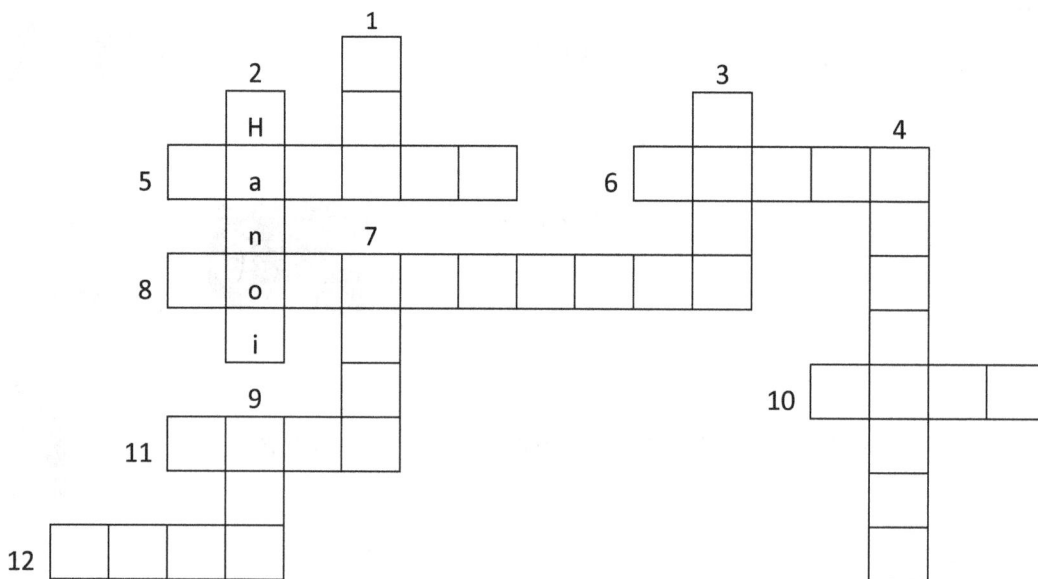

Read and listen to the story about 'Choy's foil toys'.

Comprehension questions:

1. Where did Choy live as a boy? _____

2. What jobs has Choy done during his life? _____

3. What are some of the things that bring joy to Choy? _____

Listen to the rhyming story about 'Choy's foil toys' again.
Write in the missing words that have the same vowel sound as 'f<u>oi</u>l t<u>oy</u>s':

Choy was born not far from Hanoi

and lived on a farm as a little _____.

He used to be a senior _____

and always a decent, fair _____.

Now he's retired, Choy _____

the pleasure and fun of making _____.

He loves to hear the playful _____

of his son's young, active, boisterous_____.

He remembers his days as a little _____

when he didn't own a single_____.

He watched his parents work and_____

growing soy and rice in dark, moist _____.

When he grew to an older_____

he lived with his uncle in_____.

He worked in a factory making_____

into cans and tubes and long thin_____.

Then Choy was encouraged by his _____

to go and study to be a _____.

He studied hard, and was soon _____

in a job doing work he quite _____.

Now he's retired, he makes lots of _____

from paper and foil for girls and _____.

He also enjoys growing things in the_____;

especially the soy beans he makes into_____.

It's a time of life he truly _____,

spending time with his children's girls and_____.

Making boats and planes, just simple _____,

for Choy, is one of life's great _____.

Spelling and pronunciation practice

One word in each line <u>doesn't</u> have the same vowel sound as 'foil'? Circle the different word.

1.	toy	top	boy	soy
2.	boys	poise	noise	nose
3.	sort	soil	oil	coil
4.	toil	foil	job	joy

Answers, page 102.

Spelling lists – Words with the vowel sound in ' f<u>oi</u>l t<u>oy</u>s'

- Read through the **'Choy's foil toys'** story again.

- Find all the words with the same vowel sound as in **'f<u>oi</u>l'**. (There are more than 20 words.)

- Write the words that you find in the story with the vowel sound in **'f<u>oi</u>l'** in the columns below.

- Put the words in the columns according to the spelling pattern.
  You can check you have the correct words in the correct column by checking 'Spelling Reference Lists' at the back of the **Rhyming Stories** book (p. 92).

oi	oy
Hanoi	Choy

Write words for things on the **'Choy's foil toys'** picture page (page 36 of the 'Rhyming Stories' storybook) with the vowel sound in **f<u>oi</u>l**. There are more than 6 words.

oi	oy
foil	Choy

Speaking activity - ask three people the questions below and write short answers.

Survey questions	Name:	Name:	Name:
1. What was your favourite childhood toy?			
2. Have you ever made a simple child's toy?			
3. Have you tried doing origami? (the art of paper folding)			

Research

Do you know how to make an origami boat from folded paper? Find instructions on the internet and have a competition to see who, of your friends, can create a floating paper boat first.

Using an apostrophe correctly

- An apostrophe is a small mark ' that indicates where letters are omitted when two words are joined.

    For example: he's = he is   don't = do not   I'm = I am   wasn't = was not

    In other words, an apostrophe shows where a letter is missing in 'contracted' words.

- An apostrophe also shows ownership or relationship to someone or something.

    For example: 'Choy's foil toys' means the toys belong to Choy or were made by Choy.

    'Climate change is the world's major challenge' means the challenge relates to the world.

Practice (Answers, page 102.)

The following sentences are from the 'Choy's' story. Each sentence has one or more words with an apostrophe. Read 'Choy's foil toys' again to find the words with an apostrophe, then complete the six sentences below:

1. Now _____ retired, Choy enjoys the pleasure and fun of making toys.

2. He loves to hear the playful noise of his _____ young, active, boisterous boys.

3. He remembers his days as a little boy when he _____ own a single toy.

4. Now _____ retired, he makes lots of toys from paper and foil for girls and boys.

5. _____ a time of life he truly enjoys, spending time with his _____ girls and boys.

6. Making boats and planes, just simple toys, for Choy, is one of _____great joys.

Put the words from above with an apostrophe in the correct column according to its usage.

apostrophe showing a missing letter in a contraction	apostrophe showing ownership or relationship
he's - means: he is....	son's - means: the boys belong to his son

Rhyming Stories – Language activities for 'Mike's bright lime kite'
Words that have the same vowel sound as 'br**igh**t l**i**me'

Write the words in the box next to their meaning, then write them in the crossword

bright	airline	alike ✓	cycle	dined	design	lime	kite
sights	shiny	smile	height	hike	style	delighted	

1. a high place, elevation - _____

2. having similar opinions and qualities - _____alike_____

3. places of interest to tourists - _____

4. a company that provides regular air fights by plane - _____

5. a frame covered with material that is flown in the air from a long string - _____

6. to take a long walk in the countryside - _____

7. a particular type, shape or design of something - _____

8. full of colour and light - _____

9. a light, bright colour between green and yellow; also a fruit - _____

10. a facial expression that shows happiness - _____

11. think about and draw plans for something that will be made - _____

12. describing something that reflects light - _____

13. ate a meal - _____

14. to ride a bicycle - _____

15. very pleased - _____

Answers, page 103.

Read and listen to 'Mike's bright lime kite'
Comprehension questions:

1. What was does Mike love doing? _____

2. How did Mike meet Di? _____

3. In what ways are Mike and Di alike? _____

4. What is Mike designing now?_____

Listen to the rhyming story again.

Write in the missing words that have the same vowel sound as 'bright lime':

When Mike was a child he lived in <u>China</u>.

Now he's a famous kite_____.

From the age of five, he played with _____,

watching them lift and fly great _____.

He was always excited by things in the_____

so he made up his mind he would learn to _____!

He studied five years and at age twenty_____

he was flying full-time with a famous_____.

He loved flying tourists, showing them_____;

especially at night over bright city_____.

That's when he met Di, while flying at _____;

They nodded and smiled, eyes shining _____.

When they finally spoke, they were quite _____.

They were very alike, they soon _____.

They both loved cycling, hiking and _____;

Di also liked kites and worked in_____.

While out one night, as they talked and_____,

Mike told Di of the kites he'd _____.

Di listened and smiled, very _____.

She wanted to help; she'd be_____!

Right now Mike's designing a new style of _____.

It glows in the dark; it's incredibly _____.

The kite he's designing is bright shiny _____.

It'll be in all stores in a very short_____.

Mike's very certain his lime kites will _____

all round the world, from Rome to _____.

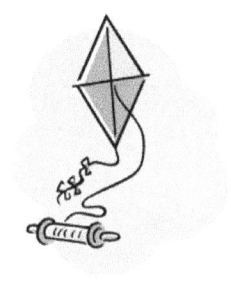

Spelling and pronunciation practice

One word in each line <u>doesn't</u> have the same vowel sound as 'lime'? Circle the different word.

1.	lime	time	white	with
2.	kite	sight	quit	quite
3.	still	smile	style	while
4.	why	sky	fill	fly

Answers, page 103.

Speaking Activity – Survey

Use the survey to find the most popular activity of those listed below:
Ask the questions and write 'yes' or 'no' answers.

Survey questions	Names									
1. Do you like flying?										
2. Do you like flying kites?										
3. Do you like hiking?										
4. Do you like cycling?										

Pronunciation of words ending with 'ed'

When words end with 'ed', usually the 'ed' is **not** pronounced as another syllable.
For example, the words 'hiked', 'wiped', 'liked' are pronounced as one syllable.

However, the letters '**ed**' always make another syllable when they are added to words ending with letters '**d**' or '**t**'.

For example: When **ed** is added to the word **end** ⟶ en**d**ed is pronounced as 2 syllables.
When **ed** is added to the word **wait** ⟶ wai**t**ed is pronounced as 2 syllables.

Write the following words from '**Mike's bright lime kites**', in the correct column below.

lived played excited loved nodded smiled liked worked talked dined designed wanted listened delighted	
1. 'ed' **not** pronounced as another syllable	2. 'ed' pronounced as another syllable

Answers, page 103.

Spelling lists – Words with the vowel sound in ''bright lime'

- Find at least 20 words in the story with the vowel sound in the words 'bright lime'.

- Put the words in the columns according to their spelling pattern. You can check the correct words in 'Spelling Reference Lists' at the back of the **Rhyming Stories** book (p. 93).

i	i + silent e	y	i + g (h)
child	Mike	fly	night
Also: eyes			

Write words for things on the **'Mike's bright lime kite'** picture page (page 38 of the **Rhyming Stories** storybook) with the sound in br**i**ght l**i**me. There are more than six words.

i	i + silent e	y	i + g (h)
Also: eyes			

Rhyming Stories – Language activities for 'Hair with Flair' at Mayfair Square'
Words that rhyme with 'sq<u>are</u>'

Write the words in the box next to their meaning, then write them in the crossword.

square ✓	chair	flair	pair	scared	prepare	aware
repair		their		parents	staring	
hair	millionaire		rare		spare	

1. a flat shape with four sides of equal length   -   _____square_____

2. to get things ready for something that is planned   -   _____

3. very unusual, doesn't happen often   -   _____

4. talent or natural ability to do something wonderfully well   -   _____

5. something extra or available for someone to use   -   _____

6. someone who has more than 1,000,000 of their country's currency ($ ¥ £ €)   -   _____

7. looking at something for a long time (especially when surprised or thinking)   -   _____

8. having knowledge or information about something   -   _____

9. two things or people connected   -   _____

10. fix something that is damaged, broken or not working correctly   -   _____

11. mother and father   -   _____

12. natural covering of the head   -   _____

13. worried or alarmed about something   -   _____

14. something to sit on; a seat which usually has four legs   -   _____

15. this word shows ownership; means 'belonging to them'   -   _____

Answers, page 104.

Comprehension questions:

1. What did Sarah and Clare both have a flair for?_____

2. What did they need to do and buy before they could begin their business? _____

_____

3. What has been the result of their new business?_____

Listen to the rhyming story again.
Write in the missing words that have the same vowel sound as 'sq<u>uare</u>':

Sarah and Clare are a talented _____

who live with their parents near Mayfair_____.

They both have a flair for cutting _____

and wanted to start a business to _____.

Last year while shopping at Mayfair _____,

a window sign made them stop and _____:

> **Store for rent**
>
> **Space: 10 square**
>
> **Air-conditioned**
>
> **Needs repair**

They stood at the window thinking and _____

at all the things that would need_____.

But a chance like this was very _____

and they were a very creative_____.

They stood discussing what would go_____;

'We'll put mirrors here and chairs over _____.'

They felt excited and a little bit_____;

there was lots to buy and lots to_____ .

They talked with their parents who made them_____

they'd try to help with what cash they had_____.

They bought square mirrors, as well as _____ _____.

They bought dryers and combs and scissors, six_____.

They painted the walls with squares here and_____

then they put signs in the shopping _____.

*** ***

Soon, people were coming from _____

to be 'cut and styled' by Sarah or _____.

Everyone said with their kind of_____

they'd soon both be a young_____!

Spelling and pronunciation practice

One word in each line <u>doesn't</u> have the same vowel sound as 'sq<u>uare</u>'? Circle the different word.

1.	pair	fair	chair	car
2.	where	here	hair	flair
3.	rare	square	start	stare
4.	star	spare	their	there

Answers, page 104.

Spelling in context – pronouns and contractions

Pronouns are words such as 'he', 'she', 'they', 'we', 'their' and 'who'.

Contractions are shortened words such as didn't (did not); I'm (I am); I've (I have); we're (we are)

Contractions can follow a pronoun, for example:

'He**'s** young' rather than, '<u>He is</u> young'.

'You**'re** funny' rather than, '<u>You are</u> funny'.

'We**'re** going to win' rather than, '<u>We are</u> going to win'.

'They**'re** late' rather than ' They are late'.

The spelling of the example words above are often confused with other words that have a similar pronunciation. Look at the <u>underlined</u> words in the following sentence.

The children are over **<u>there</u>**, with **<u>their</u>** grandparents, so **<u>they're</u>** safe and happy.

If you read the above sentence aloud, you will see that '**there**', '**their**' and '**they're**' sound the same. However the words have different meanings: '**there**' means 'that place'

'**their**' shows relationship (of the children to the grandparents).

'**they're**' is the contracted form of '**they are**'

Look at the following sentences. The **bold** words may be confused because they can be pronounced similarly.

- **You're** clever because you always do **your** homework quickly. (**you're** = you are; **your** shows possession)

- I don't know **where** he's going but **we're** supposed to be following him.
  (**where** means 'which place'; **we're** = we are (Note: we're can also be pronounced as two short syllables)

- The cat ate **its** dinner; now **it's** sitting quietly on the step. (**its** shows possession; **it's** = it is)

- **Who's** the man in the photo? He's the man **whose** house we bought. (**who's**= who is; **whose** shows ownership)

Practice

Complete the sentences below by choosing the correct word from the box and writing it in the appropriate space in the sentences (using a capital letter where necessary). The underlined pronoun in some of the sentences will give you a clue about which words to write. Answers, page 105.

They're	their	there	whose	who's	we're	were
	you're	your	it's	its (use two times)		

1) _____ very happy with <u>our</u> trip. We visited ten countries while we _____ overseas.

2) _____ much taller than _____ sister but she's older than <u>you</u>, isn't she?

3) We have a new television and _____wonderful. _____ best feature is _____ size.

4) The parents standing over _____are very happy because _____ son

   graduated from university with good results. _____ very proud parents.

5) Look! _____ that woman on television?

   She's the woman _____ cookbook I've been using.

Spelling and pronunciation - homophones

Some pairs of English words have the same pronunciation but different meanings and spelling.

For example, '**their**' which means 'belonging to them' and '**there**' meaning 'a particular place' have the same pronunciation. They are called homophones.

They're sitting over_____ and talking about _____ books.

Practice

Choose the appropriate word (from the choice given for each sentence) and complete the sentences. Use your dictionary if necessary. Answers, page 105.

1. fair/fare   I don't think it's_____ that the air_____for the trip has increased again.

2. stare/stair   The boys always_____ at each other as they sit on the _____.

3. where/wear   I don't know _____ we're going so I don't know what to _____.

Spelling lists – Words with the vowel sound in 'square'

- Find 20 words in the story about '**Hair with Flair**' with the vowel sound in the word **squa̲r̲e**.

- Put the word in the columns according to the spelling pattern. You can check the correct words in 'Spelling Reference Lists' at the back of the **Rhyming Stories** book (p. 94).

ere	ar	air	are
wh<u>ere</u>	S<u>ar</u>ah	pair	Clare

Also: their

Write words for things on the '**square**' picture page (page 40 of the Rhyming Stories storybook) with the sound in **squa̲r̲e**. There are more than six words.

ar	air	are

Words with 'silent' consonants - review

In English, many written words contain letters that are not pronounced. These letters are called 'silent' letters. For example, the letter 'b' in 'combs' is not pronounced.

There are practice activities on words with 'silent' letters on page 24 and 58 of this book. Write the words with silent letters from those pages into the lists below.

Words with 'silent' consonants

silent **w**	silent **k**	silent **b**	silent **g**	silent **l**
write	knee	climb	sign	walk

silent **t**	silent **s**	silent **n**	silent **h**	silent **g** before **h** or **th**
often	aisle	autumn	rhythm	See also page 31. might length

You can check your lists with the answers on page 105.

Answers - Words with the focus sound in 'bl<u>a</u>ck' (Dan's black hat jazz band)

1. a road vehicle used for carrying things		- van
2. thought to be important, of value, appreciated		- valued
3. the darkest colour		- black
4. a person who likes and admires a famous person		- fan
5. a group of musicians who play music together		- band
6. information that you know is true		- fact
7. a metal instrument that makes music by blowing with the mouth		- saxophone
8. very good, excellent		- fantastic
9. a soft flat hat, sometimes with an eye-shade section at the front		- cap
10. a type of music with a strong lively beat		- jazz
11. an idea of what you are going to do		- plan
12. a musical instrument like a guitar but with a round body		- banjo
13. to hit something gently with one hand or finger		- tap
14. a natural skill or ability to do something		- talent
15. hit your hands together to show you enjoyed something		- clap

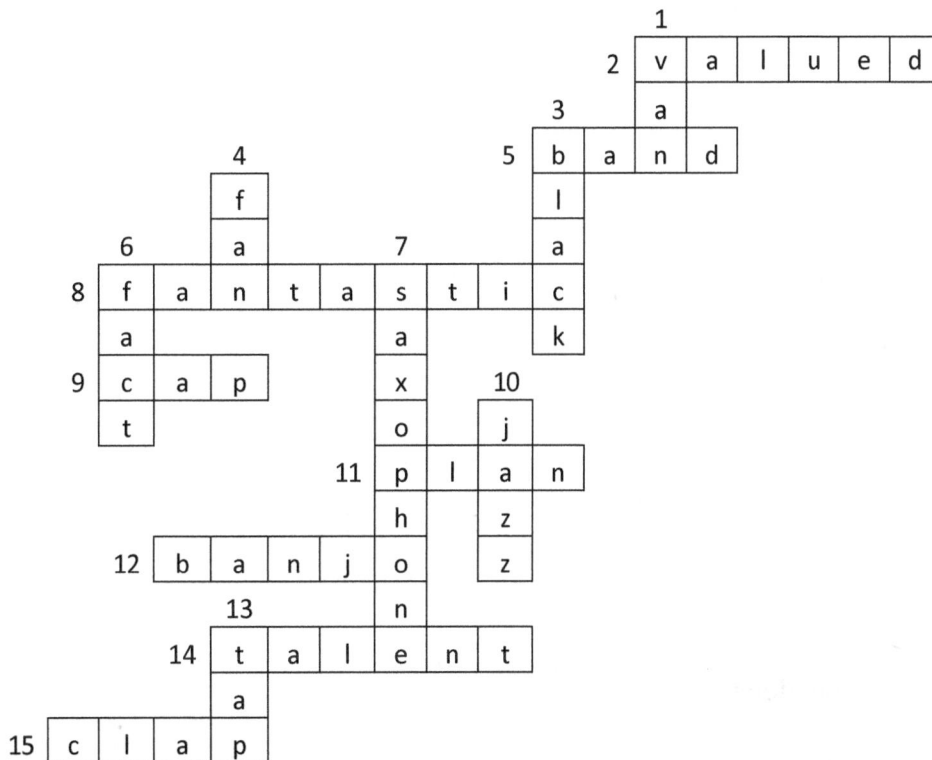

1. What kind of music does Dan play? <u>He plays fantastic jazz.</u>
2. What do Dan, Jack and Max wear when they play in their band? <u>They wear black hats or caps.</u>
3. What do people do when they hear the band? <u>They stand and everyone claps. They tap out the beat</u>
   <u>with their hands</u>

Spelling and pronunciation: The circled word in each line has a different vowel sound.

1.	v<u>a</u>n	m<u>a</u>n	(pl<u>ay</u>s)	b<u>a</u>nd
2.	(tall)	fl<u>a</u>t	bl<u>a</u>ck	h<u>a</u>t
3.	h<u>a</u>s	j<u>a</u>zz	l<u>a</u>nd	(c<u>a</u>ll)
4.	f<u>a</u>ns	(m<u>a</u>ke)	h<u>a</u>nd	cl<u>a</u>p

Pronunciation practice – Syllables

one syllable		two syllables		three syllables
black	plan	banjo	music	fantastic
band	fans	talent	travel	saxophone
hat	clap	people		understand

Answers - Words with the focus sound in 'red' (Jen, the apprentice chef)

1. an experienced cook who prepares food in a restaurant   - chef
2. a person who works for a period of time to learn a skill   - apprentice
3. unable to hear   - deaf
4. worried and not able to relax   - stressed
5. one more than six   - seven
6. unhappy about something   - up<u>set</u> (adjective)
7. think(something) may be true   - sus<u>pect</u> (verb)
8. shouted words loudly   - yelled
9. think about what the answer or result may be   - guess
10. in the place of something else   - instead
11. past verb of 'go'   - went
12. past verb of 'say'   - said
13. be very good at doing something   - excel
14. recently made, not old   - fresh
15. an examination or questions to check knowledge or ability   - test
16. a large number or amount of something   - many

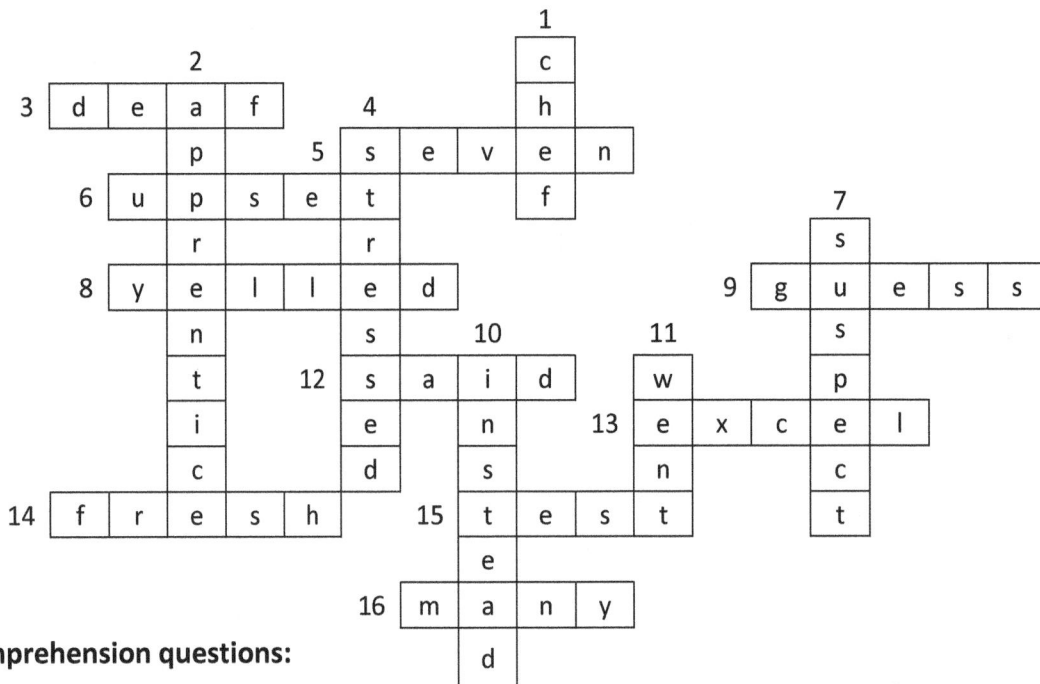

Crossword:

Across/Down answers as filled:
- 1 (down): c h e f
- 2 (down): a p p r e n t i c
- 3 (across): d e a f
- 4 (down): s t r e s s e d
- 5 (across): s e v e n
- 6 (across): u p s e t
- 8 (across): y e l l e d
- 9 (across): g u e s s
- 7 (down): s s p e c t
- 10 (down): i n s t
- 11 (down): w e n
- 12 (across): s a i d
- 13 (across): e x c e l
- 14 (across): f r e s h
- 15 (across): t e s t
- 16 (across): m a n y

Comprehension questions:

1. What did Jen <u>not</u> suspect about her health?   <u>She didn't suspect that she was deaf.</u>

2. What did Jen give Jeff when he asked for seven eggs?   <u>Chicken legs</u>

3. What did Jen do when Jeff said he thought she was deaf   <u>She went and had many tests.</u>

4. What was the result of Jen's next cooking test?   <u>Jen had done better than all the rest.</u>

The circled word in each line has a different vowel sound.

1.	deaf	(hear)	get	stressed
2.	chef	went	(her)	test
3.	(he)	ten	fresh	eggs
4.	seven	red	pens	(please)

Spelling - homophones

On the farm, we <u>bred</u> sheep for wool and cows for milk. We also made our own <u>bread</u>.

1. Have you <u>guessed</u> who is going to be the special <u>guest</u> at the party tonight?
2. Yesterday he <u>read</u> every story in the book with the <u>red</u> cover.
3. My friend <u>sent</u> me a birthday card and some expensive <u>scent</u> in a beautiful bottle.
4. The TV report didn't show <u>whether</u> tomorrow's <u>weather</u> will be hot or cold!

Answers - Words with the focus sound in 'S<u>o</u>me b<u>u</u>bble-g<u>u</u>m f<u>u</u>n'

1. a ball of air or gas inside a thin covering of liquid or gum	-	bubble
2. soft, sticky elastic material (often found in trees or plants)	-	gum
3. not old	-	young
4. speak in a way that gives someone confidence to do something	-	encourage
5. something that is necessary	-	a must
6. a place that is the centre of an activity	-	hub
7. a fully grown person	-	adult
8. to make a tune or music without opening your mouth	-	hum
9. unhappy or sad	-	glum
10. an organisation for people who want to share a social activity	-	club
11. this word can mean 'things', 'thoughts' or 'ideas'	-	stuff
12. habits, traditions or ways of behaving	-	customs
13. worry or anxiety about unimportant things	-	fuss
14. problems	-	troubles
15. difficult, unfair, not easy ('rough' can have a similar meaning)	-	tough
16. unfriendly	-	gruff

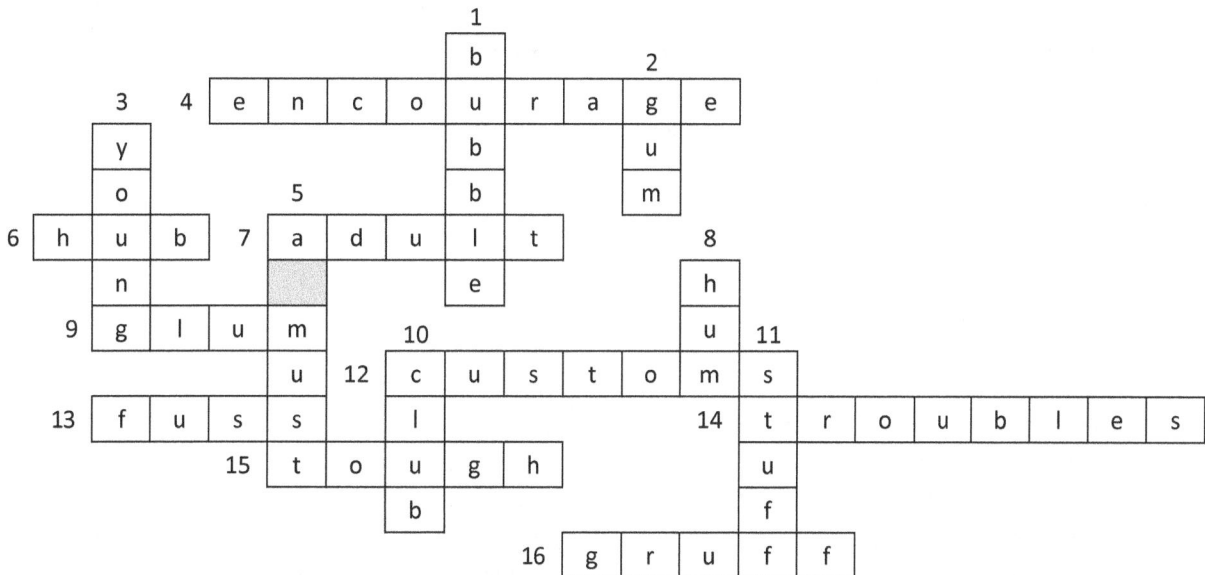

(crossword grid)

1 b
4 e n c o u r a g e — 2 (across)
b | g
3 y | b | u
o | 5 | b | m
6 h u b | 7 a d u l t | 8
n | e | h
9 g l u m | 10 | u | 11
u | 12 c u s t o m s
13 f u s s | l | 14 t r o u b l e s
15 t o u g h | u
b | f
16 g r u f f

Comprehension questions:

1. Where do Justin and Honey live? <u>They live with their father and mother</u>

2. What did Justin's mum say he <u>didn't</u> need to have fun? <u>He didn't need much money.</u>

3. What did Honey and Justin's mum encourage them to start? <u>A club which they called 'Bubble-gum Hub'</u>

4. What was the purpose of the 'Bubble-gum Hub? <u>Share customs and music and have discussions.</u>

The circled word has a different vowel sound.

1.	young	(your)	tough	rough
2.	(song)	some	stuff	gum
3.	come	some	(both)	done
4.	run	(do)	jump	hum

Consonant clusters at the beginning of words

<u>s</u> <u>w</u> <u>i</u> <u>n</u> g   <u>gr</u>apes   <u>st</u>ar   <u>cl</u>ock   <u>tr</u>ee   <u>br</u>ush (or <u>br</u>oom)   <u>fr</u>og

More words in the 'Some bubble fun' story with the same consonant clusters.

great   studied   clever   brother   troubles   friends
gruff   stuff   club   breathe

Practice with consonant clusters - Words <u>beginning</u> with the letters **str**, **scr** or **spr**?

straight	**str**ing	**str**uggle	**scr**oll	**scr**ape	**spr**ays	**spr**ig (or sprigs)
strike	stroke	strongest	scream	scratch	spring	spree
street	stray (or strays)	stroll	scrub	screw	sprinkle	
stretch	stream	stress	screen		spread	
strip	strict					

w	v	s	t	r	a	i	g	h	t	w	s	c	r	e	a	m	b
y	n	b	s	c	r	o	l	l	y	s	c	r	a	t	c	h	o
x	p	s	t	r	e	a	m	z	s	c	r	a	p	e	h	v	l
z	s	t	r	i	n	g	k	w	x	r	e	m	s	n	g	s	s
s	t	r	e	t	c	h	r	p	t	e	w	s	t	r	i	c	t
p	r	a	s	t	r	u	g	g	l	e	q	t	r	v	y	r	r
r	i	y	s	p	r	e	e	x	p	n	w	z	i	t	f	u	e
i	p	s	t	r	o	k	e	h	s	b	r	x	k	l	m	b	e
g	x	w	s	t	r	o	l	l	v	s	p	r	e	a	d	w	t
s	p	r	i	n	k	l	e	x	s	p	r	i	n	g	v	g	x
n	o	s	p	r	a	y	s	h	s	t	r	o	n	g	e	s	t

Answers – Ways of spelling the consonant sound /f/

All the words contain the consonant sound /f/ but are written with 'f', 'ph' or 'gh'.

1. not costing any money – free
2. enjoyment or pleasure - fun
3. you use a camera to make one of these - photograph
4. a person does this when something is funny - laughs
5. the people who are related to you - family
6. relating to the body - physical
7. people walk on these - feet
8. a very large animal with a long nose - elephant
9. used to speak over long distances - phone
10. not smooth - rough
11. a very thin booklet that gives information - pamphlet
12. images shown on a computer screen - graphics
13. not too much and not too little but… - enough

(crossword puzzle)

1 down: free
2 across: fun
3 down: photo
4 down: laughs
5: e
6 across: physical
7 across: feet
8: e
9 down: pamphlet / phone
10 across: rough
11 across: pamphlet
12 across: graphics
13 across: enough

Ways of spelling the consonant sound 'f'

f	ph		gh
<u>f</u>ather	<u>ph</u>otocopy	pam<u>ph</u>let	tou<u>gh</u>
<u>f</u>ree	<u>ph</u>otogra<u>ph</u>	gra<u>ph</u>ics	lau<u>gh</u>s
<u>f</u>un	<u>ph</u>ysical		rou<u>gh</u>
<u>f</u>amily	ele<u>ph</u>ant		enou<u>gh</u>
<u>f</u>eet	<u>ph</u>one		

Answers - Words with the focus sound in 'Connie's orange spot coffee shop'

1. exchange something for something else - swap
2. on the opposite side - across
3. describing something that is well made and of a good standard - quality
4. people with medical qualifications whose job is to treat sick patients - doctors
5. a choice - option
6. a small clock, usually worn on a person's wrist - watch
7. a large building with offices - block
8. to hope to have or do something - want
9. a place where you can buy things (noun); to buy things (verb) - shop
10. without stopping, continually happening - non-stop
11. everything that you need or want - the lot
12. small white bubbles on the top of liquid - froth
13. not right or not correct - wrong
14. many, a large number of people or things - lots
15. regularly, frequently - often

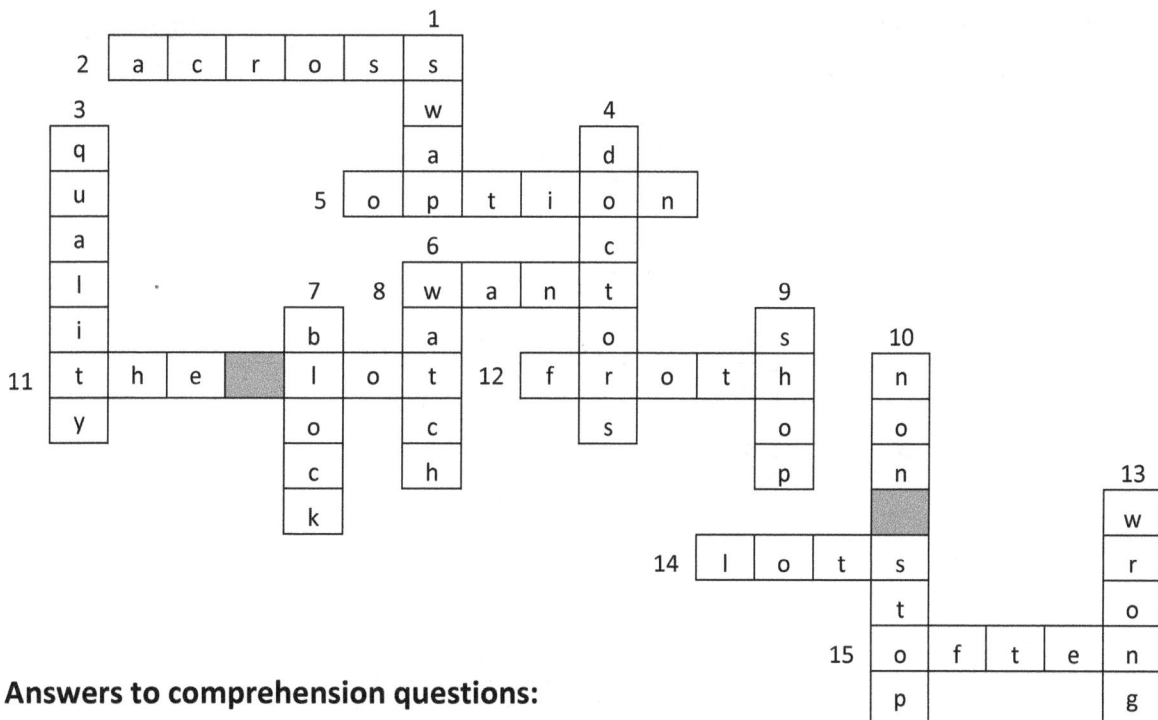

Answers to comprehension questions:

1. Where is Connie's coffee shop?   It's across the road from a parking lot and near a doctor's block.

2. What can shoppers buy at Connie's shop?
Shoppers can buy coffee, chocolate, orange cake and quality gifts such as coffee pots, bottles, clocks, watches and orange boxes.

The circled word on each line has a different vowel sound.

1. shop top (love) stop
2. got (goes) wrong want
3. what hot (short) long
4. strong (so) box pot

Answers - Pronunciation of the consonant letter 's' as /s/ or /z/

Words with the letter 's' pronounced as sound /s/	Words with the letter 's' pronounced as sound /z/
1) strong 4) soft 2) swap 5) spot 3) song 6) stop	1) was 4) goes 2) his 5) does 3) hers 6) has

Answers - Words with the focus sound in 'Ch<u>ar</u>lie's m<u>ar</u>ble c<u>ar</u>ving'

1. very hard rock with a pattern of lines through it   -   marble
2. a place or event where people buy and sell   -   market
3. the activity of painting, carving or making music etc.   -   art
4. an enclosed area of land with flowers, trees or play area   -   park
5. clever, intelligent, thinking creatively   -   smart
6. carry or take something somewhere (with effort involved)   -   cart
7. a tree with long green leaves; it grows well in warm places   -   palm
8. fifty per cent   -   half
9. land where vegetables, fruit or animals are produced as a business -   farm
10. an activity needing skill; related to making things   -   craft
11. the shape and place representing love and strong feelings   -   heart
12. big   -   large
13. peaceful, quiet and still   -   calm
14. the level or situation you want to achieve; a goal   -   target
15. cut a design into the surface or make a shape from stone or marble -   carve

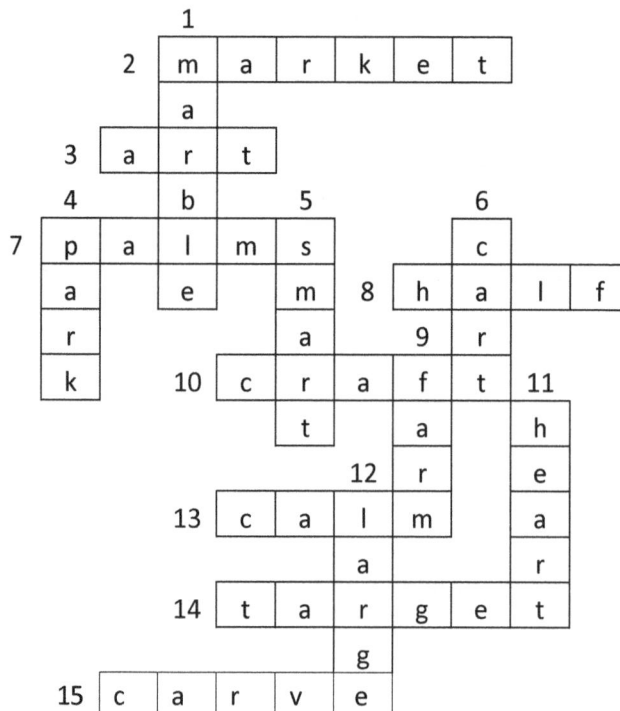

		1							
	2	m	a	r	k	e	t		
		a							
3	a	r	t						
4		b		5			6		
7	p	a	l	m	s			c	
	a		e		m	8	h	a	l	f
	r				a		9	r	
	k		10	c	r	a	f	t	11
				t		a			h
					12	r			e
		13	c	a	l	m			a
					a				r
		14	t	a	r	g	e	t	
					g				
	15	c	a	r	v	e			

Comprehension questions:

1. Where is Martin and Charlie's farm?   It's half an hour by car from Darwin.

2. What do Martin and Charlie grow on their farm?   They grow bananas, guavas, avocados and palms.

3. What does Charlie want to do more of in the future? He wants to carve beautiful things out of marble for

                                                                         parks and gardens.

Spelling and pronunciation practice

The circled word has a different vowel sound.

1.	farm	(fruit)	car	park
2.	hard	calm	(can)	carve
3.	(all)	palm	smart	art
4.	stars	heart	cart	(back)

Words with 'silent letters'

1.	from another country or another place	foreign
2.	frequently	often*
3.	sixty minutes	hour
4.	have information in your mind	know
5.	fifty per cent	half
6.	a strong, tall piece of stone or wood used to support a building	column
7.	a young cow	calf
8.	land surrounded by water	island
9.	a tree with long green leaves; it grows well in warm places	palm
10.	to hear and give attention when someone speaks	listen
11.	peaceful, quiet and still	calm
12.	words containing the same sounds	rhyme

Note: The word 'often' is usually pronounced with a silent 't', though some speakers pronounce the sound 't' in this word.

Answers - Words with the focus sound in 'N**i**ck's p**i**nk g**y**m'

1. a regular pattern of music or sound   -   rhythm
2. having a healthy weight; to be thin, but not too thin   -   slim
3. making a structure from brick, wood or metal   -   building
4. to quickly close and open one eye to show friendliness or approval   -   wink
5. a strong feeling of joy or pleasure   -   thrill
6. a meal that you take with you to eat outside   -   picnic
7. very skilled and clever   -   brilliant
8. to stop doing something   -   quit
9. a person who plays music   -   musician
10. to move something, such as a ball, with your foot   -   kick
11. attractive and pleasant to look at   -   pretty
12. food that is prepared as part of a meal   -   dish
13. an informal restaurant   -   bistro
14. an idea or mental picture of something that is possible   -   vision
15. a building with equipment for doing exercises   -   gym
16. the usual thing   -   typical

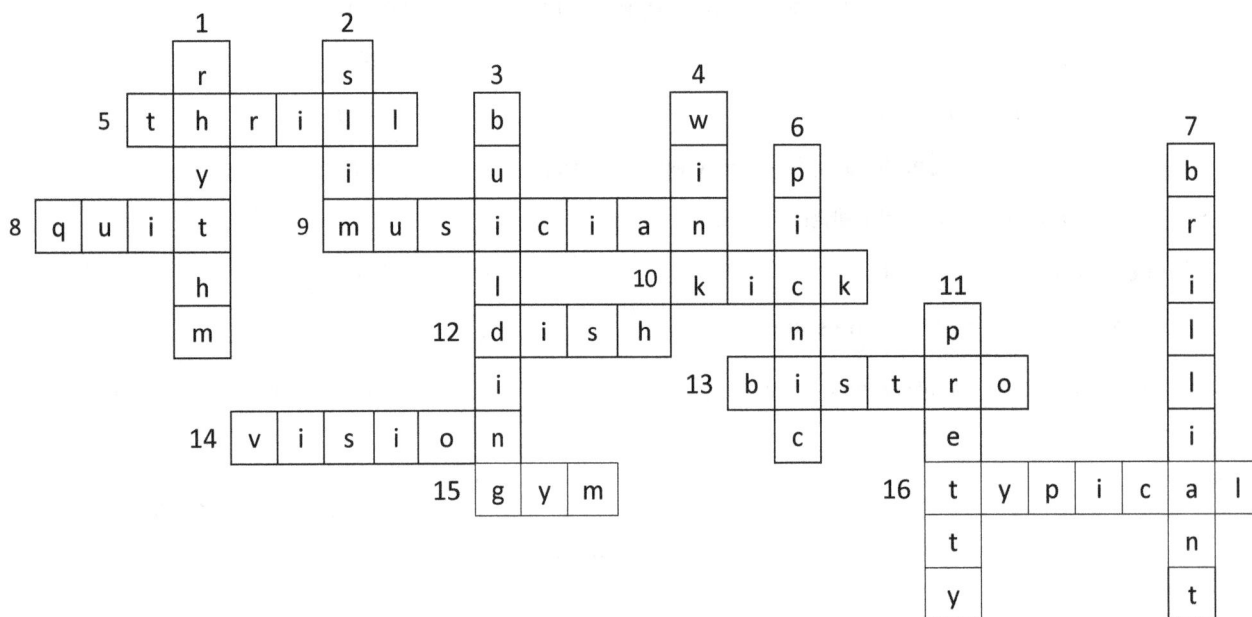

Crossword:

- 1 (down): r y t h m
- 2 (down): s i i
- 3 (down): b u i l d i n g
- 4 (down): w i n
- 5 (across): t h r i l l
- 6 (down): p i n c
- 7 (down): b r i l l i a n t
- 8 (across): q u i t
- 9 (across): m u s i c i a n
- 10 (across): k i c k
- 11 (down): p r e t t y
- 12 (across): d i s h
- 13 (across): b i s t r o
- 14 (across): v i s i o n
- 15 (across): g y m
- 16 (across): t y p i c a l

Comprehension questions:

1. What was Nick's vision? Nick's vision was to build a big gym; something different, not a typical gym.

2. What are some things Kim pictured in Nick's gym? Kim pictured a garden with a pond and a bridge and some fish and a bistro that serves a good, healthy dish; a place where children could play and kick and families could sit and have a picnic. She pictured friends meeting to listen to music. She pictured the gym painted bright pink.

The (circled) word on each line has a different vowel sound.

1.	slim	sit	(site)	still
2.	quit	(quite)	quick	fit
3.	bridge	dish	fish	(friend)
4.	(high)	hill	build	thrill

The consonant letter 'g' can be pronounced in different ways:

Words with the letter 'g' pronounced as the first sound in 'go'	Words with the letter 'g' pronounced as the first sound in 'gym'	Words with 'g' as a 'silent letter'
1) good 2) agree 3) grow 4) grin 5) go 6) garden	7) gym 8) gem 9) gentle 10) imagine 11) bridge 12) general	13) light 14) right 15) designer 16) high

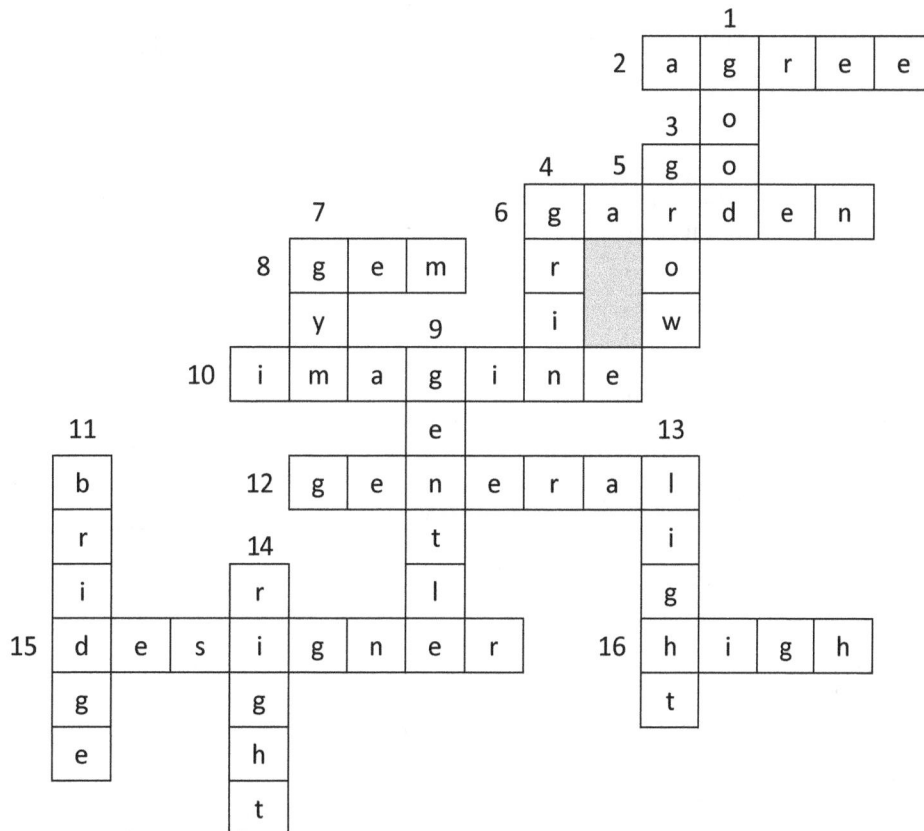

Examples of word to demonstrate guidelines for pronouncing 'g':

'g' pronounced as in **'go'**: goal , gobble, goggle, golden, goose, gossip

'g' pronounced as in **'gap'**: gabble, gallery, gallop, gang, gather

'g' pronounced as in **'gun'**: gull, gulp, gush, guts, gutter, guy

'g' pronounced as in 'glass' and 'grass' when followed by a consonant letter, such as gl…, gr…., :

gl… :   glad, glee, glow, globe,   glue, glum

gr… : grab, grace, grade, graph, gravity, green, grill, grub

g pronounced as the first sound in 'gym': gymnastics, gypsy, gypsum, gyrate; gel, gender, general, generous

*Always check a dictionary to see how words are pronounced, if in doubt.

g as a silent letter:

bright, flight, might, night, sight, tight
eight, weigh, weight

Answers - Words with the focus sound in 'Good books about wood and cooking'

1. a sweet, soft cooked dessert dish, made with rice, flour or bread — <u>pudding</u>
2. a sweetener, obtained from a plant — <u>sugar</u>
3. a word used to give advice — <u>should</u>
4. an adult female — <u>woman</u>
5. the soft thick covering on sheep; the thick thread made from this — <u>wool</u>
6. these are put on chairs to give more comfort — <u>cushions</u>
7. sweet biscuits — <u>cookies</u>
8. used with a verb to show what or is was possible — <u>could</u>
9. attractive — <u>good-looking</u>
10. past tense of 'shake' — <u>shook</u>
11. this comes from trees and is used to make buildings — <u>wood</u>
12. past tense verb of 'stand' — <u>stood</u>

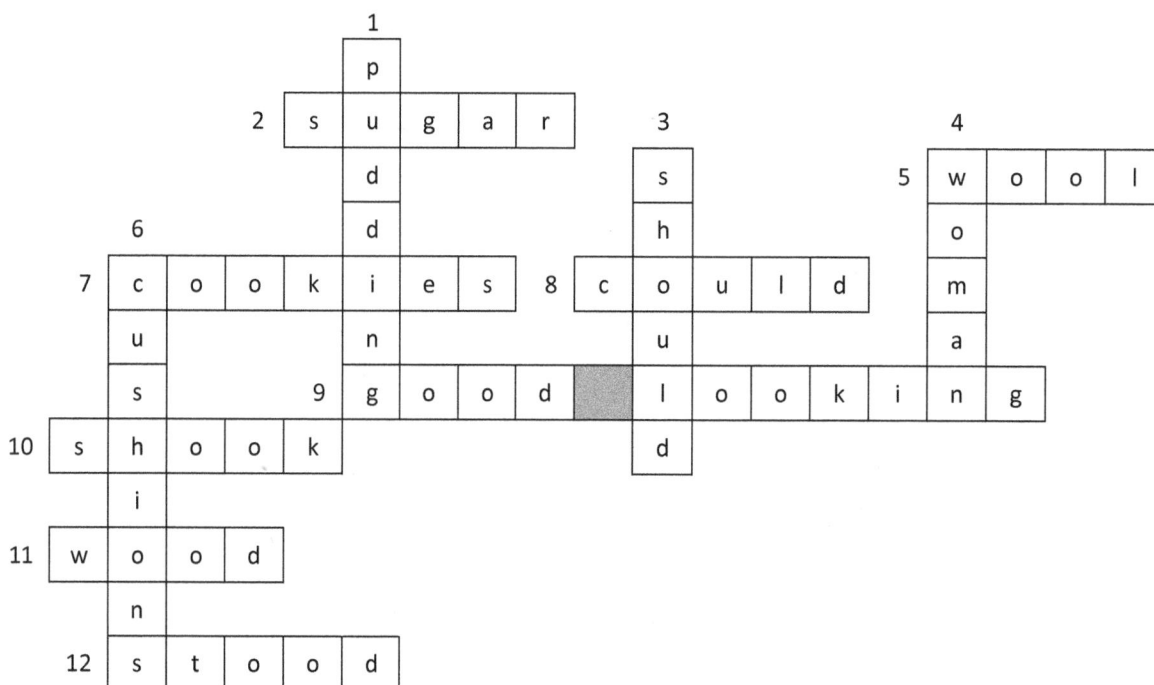

Crossword:

```
                1
                p
        2 s u g a r        3              4
                d          s         5 w o o l
        6       d          h             o
    7 c o o k i e s   8 c o u l d         m
      u       i          u               a
      s       9 g o o d [ ] l o o k i n g
10 s h o o k            d
      i
11 w o o d
      n
    12 s t o o d
```

Comprehension questions:

1. What kind of books does Brook enjoy and sell? <u>Brook likes popular fiction and books on cooking and gardening. She sells books on wood, wool and cooking.</u>

2. How is Brook's friend, Anouk described? <u>She's a good looking woman and a very good cook.</u>

3. Why did Abdul phone the bookshop? <u>He asked for a book about 'Cooking with wood'; he wanted to buy it as soon as he could.</u>

4. What happened when Abdul saw Anouk? <u>He couldn't stop staring. His heart was beating and both his knees shook; he'd marry this woman, whatever it took!</u>

The (circled) word on each line has a different vowel sound.

1.	wool	(work)	wood	stood
2.	good	cook	could	(call)
3.	put	(phone)	took	look
4.	would	should	book	(soon)

Answers - Words with the focus sound in 'Sh<u>ir</u>ley's p<u>ur</u>ple b<u>ir</u>thday'

1. a small bag or case for carrying money	-	purse
2. to be useful and beneficial	-	worthwhile
3. to be sure about something	-	certain
4. a doctor who is trained to perform medical operations	-	surgeon
5. a small book for regularly writing things that happen	-	journal
6. gets knowledge or skill in a new subject	-	learns
7. patterns of curved or circular lines	-	swirls
8. more difficult or more unpleasant than before	-	worse
9. pieces of clothing for the top part of the body	-	shirts
10. someone whose job is to care for sick or injured people	-	nurse
11. a plant that has narrow leaves and no visible flowers	-	fern
12. to be in pain or injured	-	hurt
13.to go around something, forming a circle around it	-	encircle
14. different forms or varieties of something	-	versions

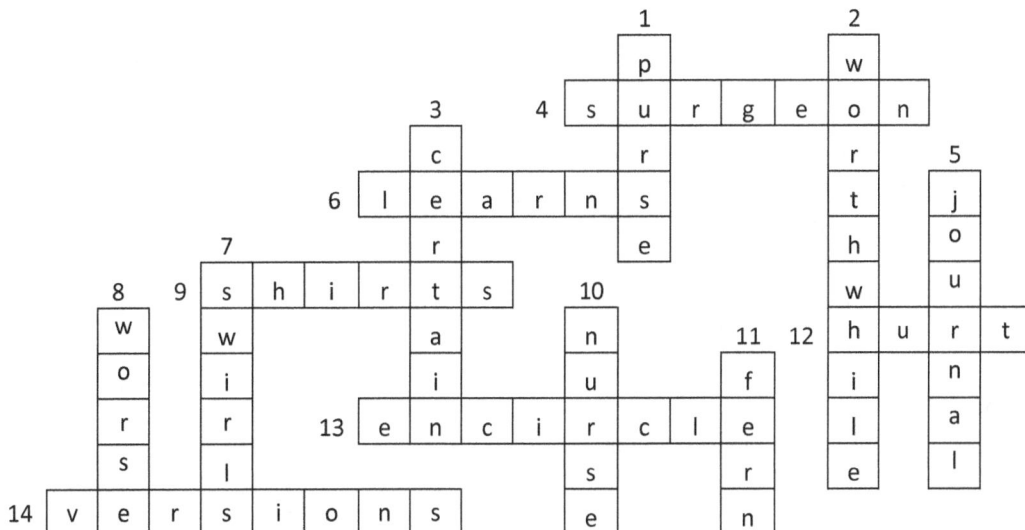

Comprehension questions:

1. What does Shirley love about her work?

<u>She loves observing busy surgeons use medical skill in all its versions.</u>

2. What purple things does Shirley have in her home?

<u>She has a purple journal, purple curtains, purple shirts and skirts.</u>

3. What gifts did Shirley get for her birthday?

<u>Her girlfriends gave her a pretty purse, a potted fern and purple shirts. She got some perfume and some</u>

<u>pearls and a pretty skirt with purple swirls.</u>

Answers: completed story about 'Shirley's Birthday Surprise'

Soon it's Shirley's thirtieth birthday.
It's on the <u>first</u>, which is next <u>Thursday</u>.
Her friends at work are in a <u>whirl</u>
making plans for the birthday <u>girl</u>.
But of these plans Shirley hasn't <u>heard</u>;
about her birthday, not one <u>word</u>.

... answers continued next page

Answers: completed story about 'Shirley's Birthday Surprise' ...continued

When Thursday arrived she felt quite <u>hurt</u>;
she hadn't even heard from <u>Bert</u>.
She walked into work sad and <u>uncertain</u>
not seeing her friends hidden by the <u>curtain</u>.
Then everyone called out 'Happy <u>Birthday</u>'
and produced a cake with the number <u>thirty</u>!

The (circled) word on each line has a different vowel sound.

1. learn   heard   (break)   burn
2. whirl   girl   fern   (friend)
3. shirts   skirts   (some)   swirls
4. work   (walk)   word   nurse

Words with the letter 'c' pronounced as /s/.

1. frozen water	-	ice
2. more than one mouse	-	mice
3. your brother's daughter	-	niece
4. this is taken by sick people to make them well	-	medicine
5. to move your feet and body to music	-	dance
6. past verb form of 'decide'	-	decided
7. your eyes, nose and mouth are on this	-	face
8. near or in the middle	-	central
9. a running competition to see who is fastest	-	race
10. a hundred years	-	century
11. a room where people work	-	office
12. a round shape	-	circle
13. a building where people go to watch movies	-	cinema
14. less than twice	-	once
15. people do this on special days	-	celebrate
16. pleasant and good	-	nice
17. a popular food in Asia	-	rice
18. a part of something such as cake or cheese	-	piece
19. the last month of the year (Use a capital letter.)	-	December
20. a very large town	-	city

Answers - Words with the focus sound in 'Gr**ee**n f**ie**lds and cl**ea**n b**ea**ches'

1. the smallest amount or minimum - least
2. a food that is made from milk; it can be soft or hard - cheese
3. happy about a situation - pleased
4. to think that something is true - believe
5. a country in southern Europe - Greece
6. important qualities or parts of something - features
7. the explanation or facts about why something is true - reason
8. the top of a mountain - peak
9. the daughter of your brother or sister - niece
10. to have the same opinion as someone - agree
11. describing the side of a mountain with a sharp upward angle - steep
12. opposite direction to 'west' - east
13. travelled over snow with special equipment on your feet - skied
14. describing a naturally beautiful scene or place - scenic
15. very interested in something or someone - keen on
16. describing a kind, attractive person - sweet

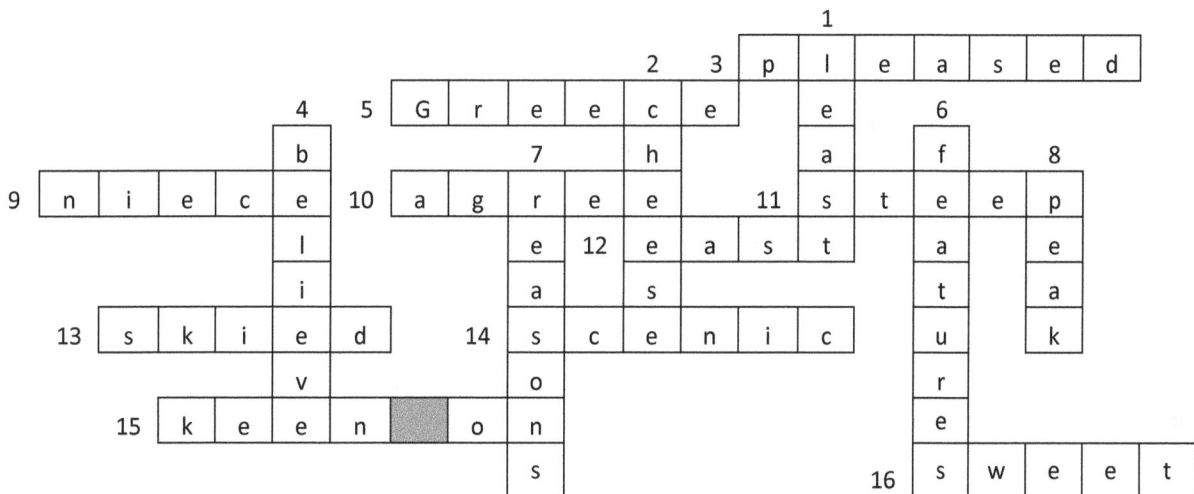

Comprehension questions:

1. What has Gina seen in New Zealand? She's seen a lot of sheep, steep mountains and peaceful beaches.

2. Why did Steve keep eating cheese and drinking tea? He wanted to hear Gina speak of things she wanted to see.

3. Why do Dino and Nina believe they'll be seeing Gina in future seasons? She seems to be keen on Steve

The circled word on each line has a different vowel sound.

1. niece (nice) east least
2. clean (their) green tea
3. three cheese week (were)
4. beach leave ski (climb)

More examples of ' ie' spelling: piece, fields, shield, thief

Spelling and pronunciation – homophones

   She is still feeling <u>weak</u> after a <u>week</u> in bed with the flu.

1) I won't have any <u>peace</u> until I find the last <u>piece</u> of the puzzle.
2) I'll <u>meet</u> you outside the supermarket after I buy the <u>meat</u> for dinner.
3) The young boy wants a <u>real</u> fishing line and <u>reel</u> this year, in place of the fishing net he used last year.
4) The accident <u>scene</u> was the most terrible thing I have ever <u>seen</u>.
5) The <u>steel</u> bars were so heavy, nobody could <u>steal</u> them.
6) We <u>leased</u> the office for a year because it was the <u>least</u> expensive way to start our business.
7) You can <u>see</u> all the way to the <u>sea</u> from here.
8) I've <u>been</u> making <u>bean</u> soup while you've <u>been</u> sleeping.
9) 'When I reach the mountain <u>peak,</u> I'll <u>peek</u> over the top.'

More words with the sound as in 'gr<u>ee</u>n'

Suggested answers:

Things to eat:
cheese, greens, sweets, b<u>ee</u>troot peach, wheat, beans, peas, meat, cream, yeast, meals chilli, spaghetti

Places to go:	Greece, Greenland New Zealand, beach, sea, field Egypt, Sweden, Indonesia Lima, Vietnam, Sydney

Animals, insects and birds to see:
sheep, cheetah, bee, leech, eel beaver, flea, eagle, emu monkey

Answers - Words with the focus sound in 'P<u>au</u>l's c<u>or</u>k b<u>oa</u>rds'

1. 25% (twenty-five percent)   -   quarter
2. put something new somewhere and make it ready for use   -   install
3. past verb form of 'think'   -   thought
4. a flat piece of wood, cork or plastic   -   boards
5. put in a request for something you want to buy   -   order
6. past verb form of 'buy'   -   bought
7. it is certain, without any doubt   -   for sure
8. someone whose job is to report information and events   -   reporter
9. bad and unpleasant   -   awful
10. the place where two walls meet together   -   corner
11. making you feel satisfied and happy with what you've done   -   rewarding
12. light soft material obtained from a particular tree   -   cork
13. fighting between groups of people   -   war
14. a shop or warehouse where goods are sold to the public   -   store
15. not interesting   -   boring
16. the lines around the edge of something   -   borders

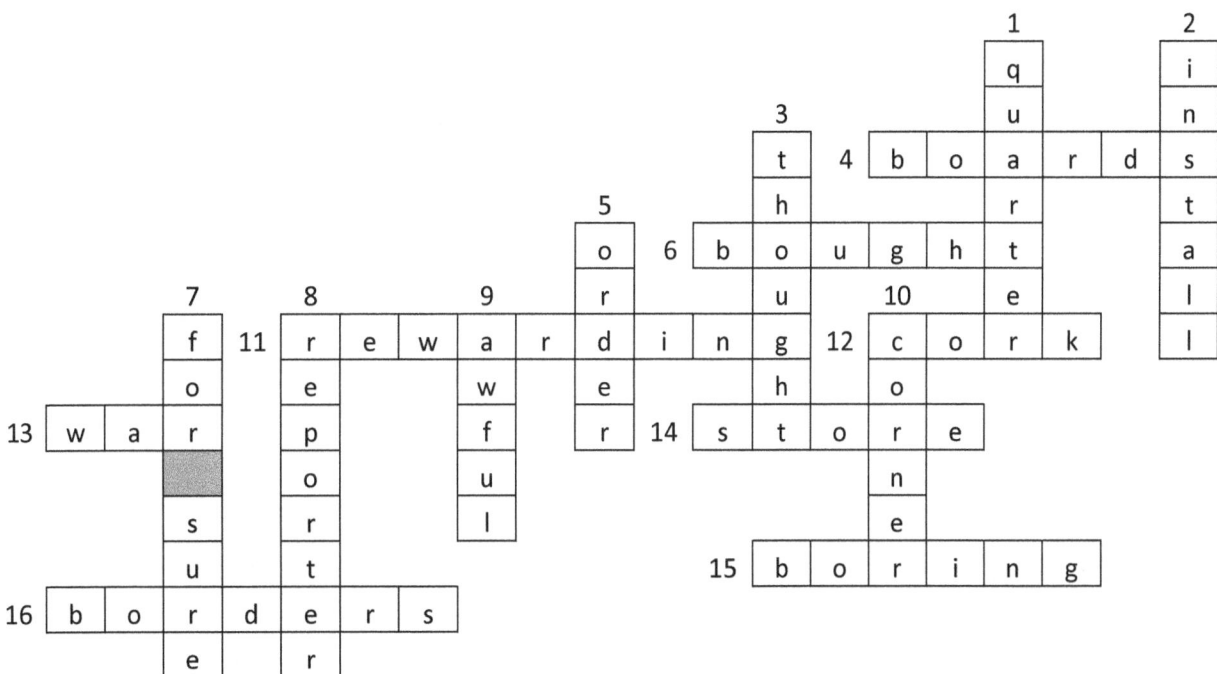

Comprehension questions:

1. What was Paul's job before and why was it awful? <u>Paul was a reporter who reported on trouble and war.</u>

2. What did Paul and Dawn put in the sports store? They installed a new door and put cork on the walls and floors. They stocked boards and balls for all sorts of sports, shorts and cork boars for the walls.

The (circled) word in each line has a different vowel sound.

1.	short	store	(work)	more
2.	call	war	wall	(are)
3.	board	(good)	door	floor
4.	saw	for	sure	(new)

Spelling and pronunciation

He was <u>bored</u> when he worked in the factory making <u>board</u>.

1. As a child I was a <u>boarder</u> at a boarding school near the northern <u>border</u> of the country.

2. They are fixing the uneven, <u>coarse</u> surface of the race<u>course</u> to make it safer for horses.

3. Environmental issues are at the <u>fore</u>front and will stay that way for the next <u>four</u> decades.

4. She's <u>mourning</u> the loss of her little dog which died yesterday <u>morning</u>.

5. 'Hold on to the <u>oar</u> tightly, <u>or</u> it will be difficult getting back to the shore.'

6. You should <u>pour</u> some warm water over the poor injured cat's sore <u>paw</u>.

7. The lions will <u>roar</u> loudly until the zookeeper gives them some <u>raw</u> meat.

8. They're <u>sure</u> they saw a large crocodile on the <u>shore</u> of the bay.

9. When I <u>saw</u> the accident victim, I knew he'd be <u>sore</u> for a long time.

10. The band <u>wore</u> uniforms when they marched to the <u>war</u> memorial.

11. 'If you don't do <u>your</u> homework <u>you're</u> going to fail the exam!'

Answers - Words with the focus sound in 'Pr<u>ue</u>'s bl<u>ue</u> m<u>u</u>sic sch<u>oo</u>l'

1. say you will not accept something - refuse
2. to have no ideas, not know or understand - no clue
3. school where students learn to give beauty treatments - beauty school
4. very large - huge
5. a plan or activity that a person follows for a period of time - pursuit
6. a teacher who teaches a student or a small group - tutor
7. unable to think clearly about something - confused
8. some people together - group
9. an expression that can mean 'wonderful, good, great' - cool
10. young people - youth
11. a room used for music, art or photography - studio
12. to decide and select which things you want - choose
13. to not have something because it's gone or lost - lose
14. from the beginning of something to the end - through
15. the things you can see - view
16. long pieces of pasta made from flour, egg and water - noodles

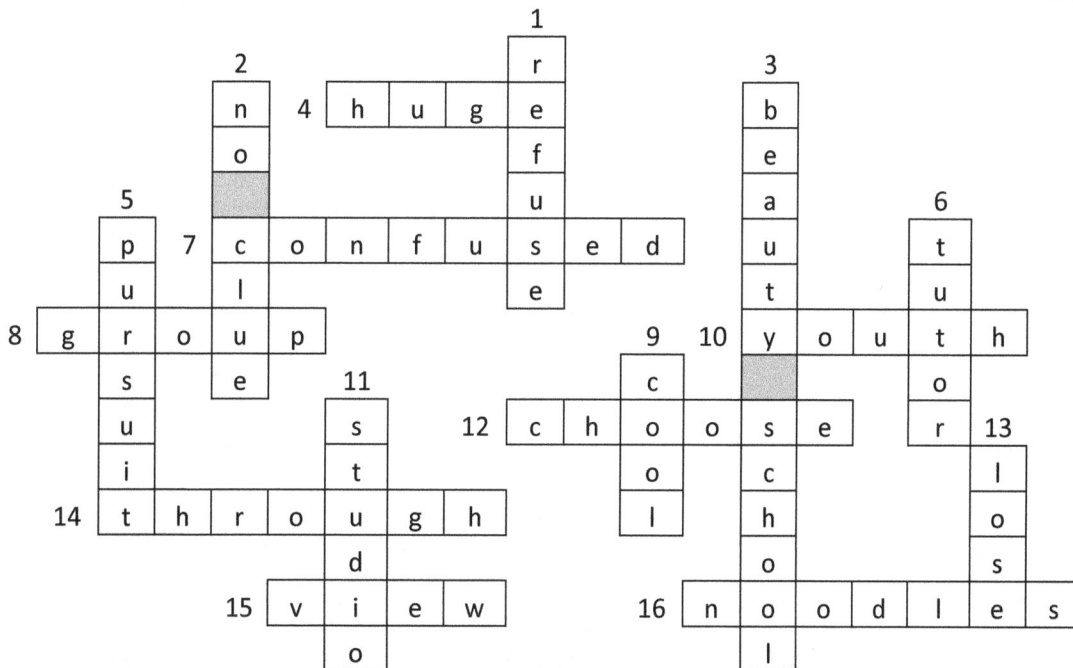

Crossword grid:

- 1 down: r e f u s e
- 4 across: h u g e
- 2 down: n o
- 3 down: b e a u t
- 5 down: p u s u i
- 7 down: c l e
- 7 across / 5: c o n f u s e d
- 8 across: g r o u p
- 9 down: c o o l
- 10 across: y o u t h
- 6 down: t u t o r
- 12 across: c h o o s e
- 11 down: s t u d
- 13 down: l o s
- 14 across: t h r o u g h
- 15 across: v i e w
- 16 across: n o o d l e s

Comprehension questions:

1. List the types of work that Prue had tried: She taught swimming, worked in a food shop, and tutored music students. She also worked in a shoe shop and a beauty school.

2. What does she really love doing? Prue loves playing music, especially the flute.

3. What did she decide to start and what will she call it? She'll start a music school and call it 'Prue's Studio Blue'.

Spelling and pronunciation practice

The (circled) word on each line has a different vowel sound.

1. (good)   school   pool   cool
2. soup   group   (young)   youth
3. true   blue   (fun)   flute
4. (could)   through   view   knew

Spelling - homophones:

The leaves **blew** off the tree in the strong wind and fell into the **blue** water.

1. My husband had the **flu** last week but he still **flew** to New York.

2. As soon as the woman saw the **new** car, they **knew** her husband would buy it.

3. When the movie producer gave the **cue**, the actors stood in the **queue.**

4. This is **too** heavy for **two** people to carry; we need more people **to** help us.

5. The boy **threw** the ball **through** the gate and into the park.

Answers - Words with the focus sound in 'H<u>ow</u>ard Br<u>own</u>'s m<u>ou</u>ntain h<u>ou</u>se'

1. feeling very pleased with something you have done	-	proud
2. there is certainty, the situation is certain, definite	-	no doubt
3. do funny things to make people laugh; to act like a clown	-	clown around
4. large groups of people	-	crowds
5. past verb form of 'find'	-	found
6. the organisation that makes decisions for a town	-	council
7. the land around a particular organisation or building	-	grounds
8. place in a bathroom where you wash by standing under a water spray	-	shower
9. tall, narrow structure or building, taller than other buildings in the area	-	tower
10. a place where people live	-	house
11. a structure in a garden or park that makes water go into the air	-	fountain
12. the colour of chocolate	-	brown
13. the look on a person's face when they are unhappy or worried	-	frown
14. a place where people live, work and shop	-	town
15. energy such as electricity that provides light and heat to buildings	-	power
16. old and in a bad condition, something that needs repairing	-	run-down

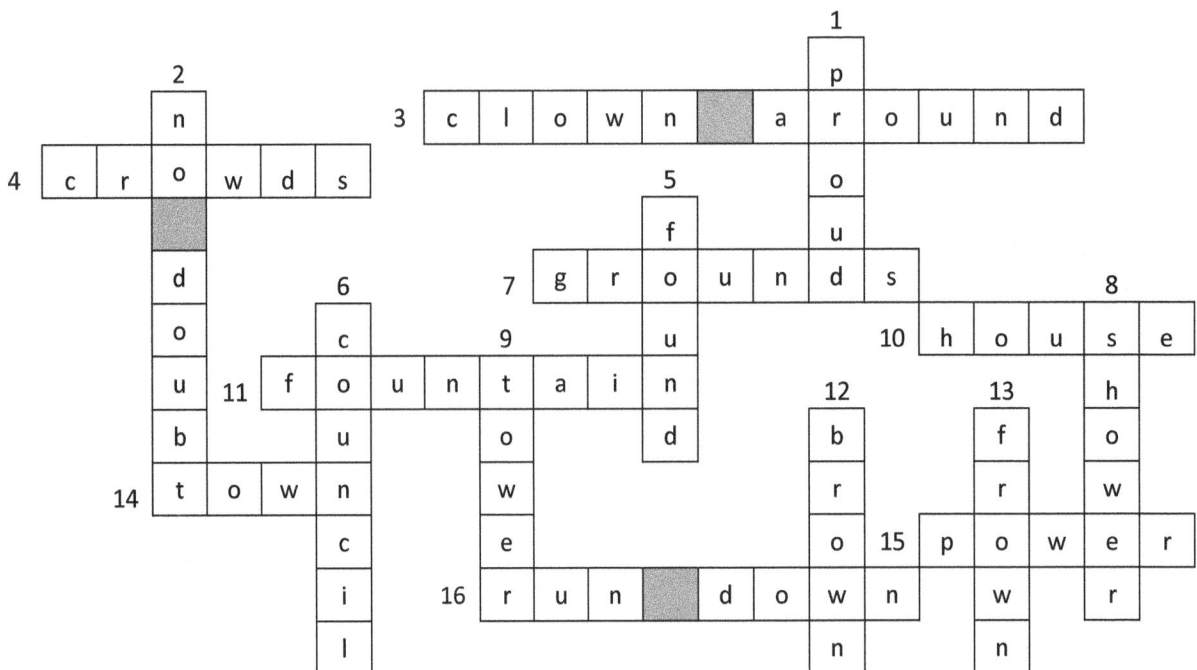

Crossword

- 1 p
- 2 n
- 3 c l o w n [ ] a r o u n d
- 4 c r o w d s
- p → r o u
- 5 f
- 7 g r o u n d s
- 9 u
- 10 h o u s e
- 11 f o u n t a i n
- 12 b r o w n
- 13 f r o w n
- 14 t o w n
- 15 p o w e r
- 16 r u n [ ] d o w n
- 6 c o u n c i l
- shower / house / brown

Comprehension questions:

1. What is Howard's job? <u>He repairs old house and works for the council maintaining the public grounds, weeding, trimming flowers, building walls and fountains.</u>

2. Why did Howard move out of town and what did he buy? <u>He moved out of town as crowds moved in. He bought an old houses that was very run-down.</u>

3. What improvements did Howard make? <u>He moved all rubbish from around the grounds and painted outside different shades of brown. He put in flowers and built a fountain.</u>

The ⟨circled⟩ word on each line has a different vowel sound.

1.	doubt	down	brown	(work)
2.	crowd	loud	(could)	ground
3.	town	house	frown	(bought)
4.	(four)	out	proud	found

Words with 'silent letters'

1. to move upward	climb	8. hit something to make a noise	knock
2. to have information	know	9. past verb for 'know'	knew
3. to put letters on paper	write	10. short finger on side of hand	thumb
4. something for your hair	comb	11. part of your leg	knee
5. a job fixing water pipes	plumber	12. something owed to someone	debt
6. not right	wrong	13. a small line or fold of the skin	wrinkle
7. not certain	doubt		

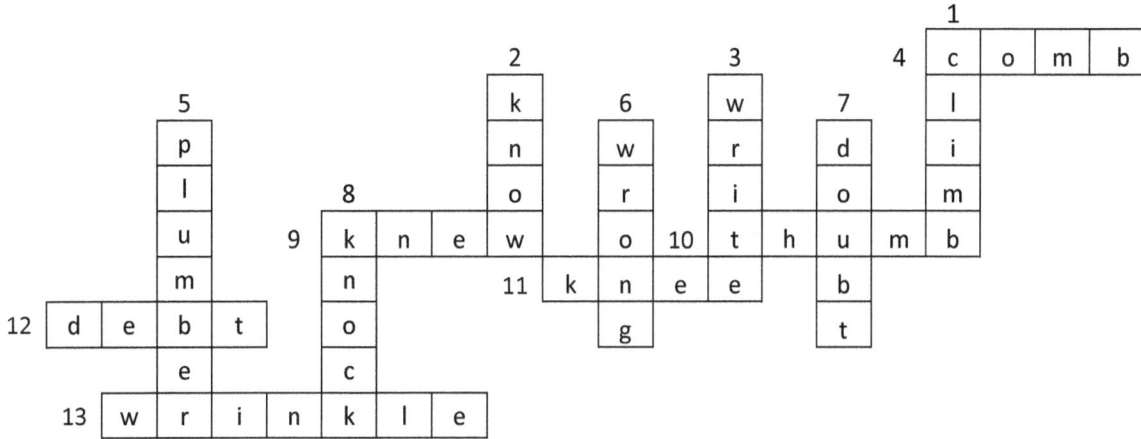

```
                                                                    1
                                                                    +---+---+---+---+
                                                                  4 | c | o | m | b |
                                                                    +---+---+---+---+
                    2               3                               | l |
                    +---+           +---+           7               | i |
                    | k |       6   | w |           +---+           +---+
                    | n |       +---+| r |           | d |          | i |
                8   | o |       | w || i |           | o |          | m |
        9  +---+---+---+---+    | r |+---+  10  +---+---+---+---+---+---+
           | k | n | e | w |    | o |    | t | h | u | m | b |
           +---+   | n |        | o |    +---+           +---+
    5              | o |    11  | k | n | e | e |        | b |
    +---+          +---+        +---+    | n |           +---+
    | p |          | c |                | e |           | t |
    | l |          +---+                | g |           +---+
    | u |
    | m |
12  +---+---+---+---+
    | d | e | b | t |
    +---+   | e |
            +---+
    13  +---+---+---+---+---+---+---+
        | w | r | i | n | k | l | e |
        +---+---+---+---+---+---+---+
```

Some patterns with the use of silent consonants.

Silent 'b' can follow	__m__	climb	comb	thumb	plumber

Silent 'b' can also go before	__t__	doubt	debt		

At the beginning of words, silent 'k' can go before	__n__	know	knew	knee	knock

At the beginning of words, silent 'w' can go before	__r__	write	wrong	wrinkle	

See page 105 for lists of words with silent letters.

Answers - Words with the focus sound in 'Gr**ey** d**ay** at the b**ay**'

1. a vacation or period of time away from work or school   -   a break
2. say that something is wrong and you are upset about it   -   complain
3. staying in a place until something happens or someone arrives   -   waiting
4. lines of water moving on the ocean's surface and on to the beach   -   waves
5. an area of natural countryside   -   landscape
6. one more than seven   -   eight
7. a hole in the side of a mountain or under the ground   -   cave
8. an area of water with land all around it   -   lake
9. activities, entertainment or sport played for fun or competition   -   games
10. the colour between black and white   -   grey
11. very good, important or famous   -   great
12. a sport using boats with sails on the water   -   sailing
13. to make pictures of places or things using paint and brushes   -   painting
14. a place where the sea is surrounded on three sides by land   -   bay

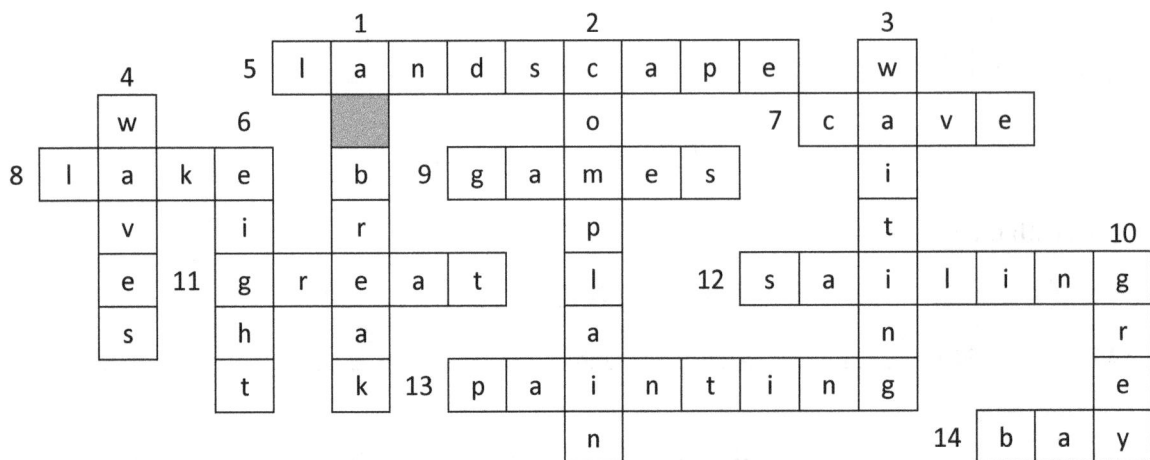

Crossword grid (answers):
- 5 (across): l a n d s c a p e
- 3 (down): w ... i t i n g (waiting)
- 4 (down): w a v e s
- 7 (across): c a v e
- 8 (across): l a k e
- 6 (down): b r e a k
- 9 (across): g a m e s
- 2 (down): c o m p l a i n
- 11 (across): g r e a t
- 12 (across): s a i l i n g
- 10 (down): g r e y
- 13 (across): p a i n t i n g
- 14 (across): b a y

Comprehension questions:

1. What plans did James and Kay make in May? They planned to go for an eight day break; to a sunny place near a beach and a lake. They'd planned to swim and surf the waves and maybe see some caves.

2. What was the weather like at Sandy Bay? The weather was cold and windy and grey.

3. What indoor activity did Kay try? She tried landscape painting.

4. What happened when Kay went back home? Eight months later Kay became a famous painter.

The (circled) word on each line has a different vowel sound.

1. great   break   (beach)   grey
2. cave   lake   wave   (when)
3. they   take   eight   (end)
4. paint   sail   (said)   rain

Spelling and pronunciation - homophones

There were eight small cakes on the plate but the boys ate them all.

1) Did you break the glass in your car brake lights when you had the accident?
2) My friend gave me a great gift for my kitchen; I use it to grate cheese and vegetables.
3) When the window pane broke I cut my hand. The pain was very bad.
4) The plane I arrived in was a plain grey colour; the seats inside were plain grey too.
5) The ship with the big sail has been for sale for eight months and I want to buy it.
6) Have you heard the tale called 'How the kangaroo got its tail'?
7) You should wait till you lose more weight before going in the race.
8) I don't want to waste this food but I want to keep a slim waist so I must stop eating.
9) The best way to weigh yourself is to do it the same time each day.

Answers - Words with the focus sound in 'G**o**lden r**o**ses, yell**ow** b**oa**ts'

1. a target, something to aim towards	-	goal
2. idea or opinion	-	notion
3. a short funny story told to make people laugh	-	joke
4. moving through the water using oars	-	rowing
5. the colour of gold, also a colour similar to yellow	-	golden
6. international, worldwide	-	global
7. take possession or management of something	-	take over
8. a short, light sleep	-	doze
9. land along the shoreline; where land and ocean meet	-	coast
10. the shortened form of 'will not'	-	won't
11. an expression meaning something 'is generally true'	-	on the whole
12. to make more known or increase sales	-	promote

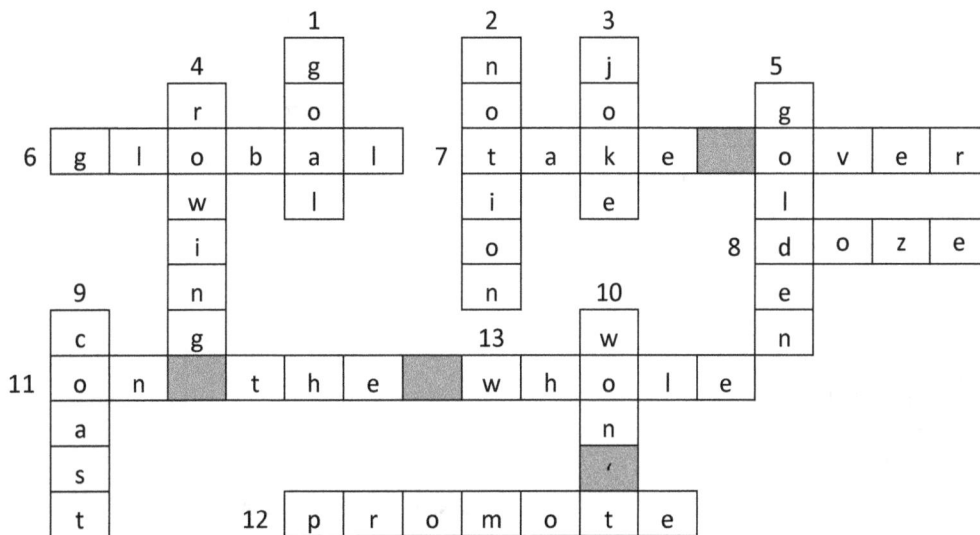

Crossword grid:

Across: 6 g l o b a l — 7 t a k e [ ] o v e r — 8 d o z e — 11 o n [ ] t h e [ ] w h o l e — 12 p r o m o t e

Down: 1 g o — 2 n o t i o n — 3 j o k e — 4 r o w i n g — 5 g o l d e n — 9 c o a s t — 10 w o n '

Comprehension questions:

1. What is Flo and Joe's business? <u>They have a business selling and renting boats. Flo also grows roses.</u>
2. What happened to Joe a month ago?
   <u>He had an accident on his (motor) bike. He hurt his nose and broke his shin bone.</u>
3. What are Flo and Joe planning now? <u>They plan to show Flo's golden roses at global shows.</u>

Spelling and pronunciation practice

The (circled) word on each line has a different vowel sound.

1.	know	(one)	snow	row
2.	hopes	home	(long)	phone
3.	coast	boat	cold	(month)
4.	road	rose	most	(son)

Spelling - homophones

There are <u>no</u> students in this class who <u>know</u> the correct answer.

1. Of all the flowers planted in <u>rows</u>, I think the <u>rose</u> looks best.
2. If you apply for <u>a loan</u> from the bank, then you <u>alone</u> should pay it back.
3. The jungle had <u>grown</u> so thick that it was very difficult to find our way. Even the experienced walkers began to <u>groan</u> with the struggle.
4. I always <u>moan</u> a lot when the grass has to be <u>mown</u>.
5. The farmer and his wife work <u>so</u> well together. He <u>sows</u> the seed while she <u>sews</u> their clothes.
6. When he <u>tows</u> the old car through the gateway, stand well back or watch your <u>toes</u>.
7. At the construction site, I spent the <u>whole</u> day digging a very large <u>hole</u>!
8. The boys <u>rowed</u> their boats along the river, while the girls <u>rode</u> their bikes along the <u>road</u>.

Answers - Words with the focus sound in 'Ch**oy**'s f**oi**l t**oy**s'

1. bean of an Asian plant that is used as food and produced as sauce   -   soy
2. Capital city of Vietnam   -   Hanoi
3. pleasures, situations or activities that make you happy   -   joys
4. someone who employs other people to work for them   -   employer
5. a person whose job is to give advice about the law   -   lawyer
6. a sound, especially one that is loud or causes disturbance   -   noise
7. the ground in which plants grow   -   soil
8. excited and lively   -   boisterous
9. a fatty liquid, thicker than water and used for cooking   -   oil
10. a long thin piece of something bent into several circular bends   -   coil
11. metal made into very thin sheets for various uses   -   foil
12. work hard   -   toil

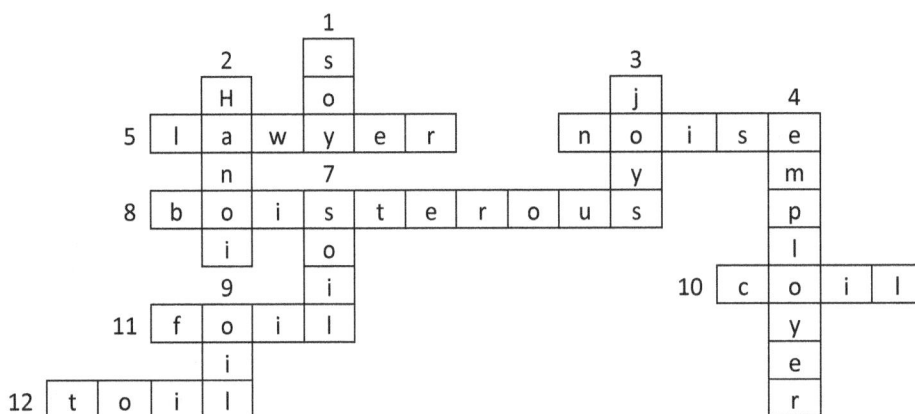

		1							3				4		
	2	s							j						
	H	o													
5	l	a	w	y	e	r		n	o	i	s	e			
	n	7							y			m			
8	b	o	i	s	t	e	r	o	u	s		p			
	i	o										l			
	9	i						10	c	o	i	l			
11	f	o	i	l					y						
	i								e						
12	t	o	i	l					r						

Comprehension questions

1. Where did Choy live as a boy? He lived on a farm near Hanoi and later with his uncle in Hanoi.

2. What jobs has Choy done during his life? He worked in a factory making foil into cans and tubes and coil.
Later, he became a senior lawyer.

3. What are some of the things that bring joy to Choy? He enjoys pending time with his grandchildren,
making simple toys from paper and foil for them. He also enjoys growing
soy beans which he makes into oil.

Spelling and pronunciation practice: The circled word on each line has a different vowel sound.

1.   toy   (top)   boy   soy
2.   boys   poise   noise   (nose)
3.   (sort)   soil   oil   coil
4.   toil   foil   (job)   joy

Using an apostrophe correctly - practice

1. Now he's retired, Choy enjoys the pleasure and fun of making toys.
2. He loves to hear the playful noise of his son's young, active, boisterous boys.
3. He remembers his days as a little boy when he didn't own a single toy.
4. Now he's retired, he makes lots of toys from paper and foil for girls and boys.
5. It's a time of life he truly enjoys, spending time with his children's girls and boys.
6. Making boats and planes, just simple toys, for Choy, is one of life's great joys.

apostrophe showing a missing letter in a contraction	apostrophe showing ownership or relationship
he's – means: he is.... didn't – means: did not... he's – means: he is... It's – means: it is...	son's –means: the boys belong to his son children's – means: the girls & boys belong to his children (They are Choy's grandchildren.) life's – means: the joys relate to Choy's life

Answers - Words with the focus sound in 'Mike's bright lime kite'

1. a high place, elevation	-	height
2. having similar opinions and qualities	-	alike
3. places of interest to tourists	-	sights
4. a company that provides regular air fights by plane	-	airline
5. a frame covered with material that is flown in the air from a long string	-	kite
6. to take a long walk in the countryside	-	hike
7. a particular type, shape or design of something	-	style
8. full of colour and light	-	bright
9. a light, bright colour between green and yellow; also a fruit	-	lime
10. a facial expression that shows happiness	-	smile
11. think about and draw plans for something that will be made	-	design
12. describing something that reflects light	-	shiny
13. ate a meal	-	dined
14. to ride a bicycle	-	cycle
15. very pleased	-	delighted

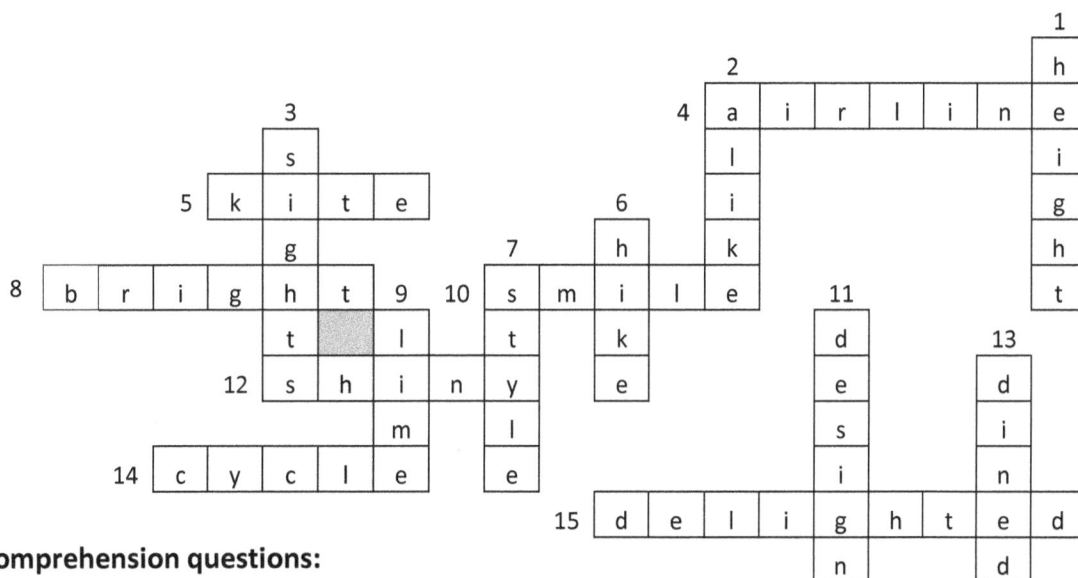

(Crossword puzzle grid with answers filled in: airline, height, sights, kite, hike, bright, smile, shiny, cycle, delighted, design, dined)

Comprehension questions:

1. What was does Mike love doing? He loves kites and flying (especially showing tourists bright city lights.

2. How did Mike meet Di? He met Di while flying at night.

3. In what ways are Mike and Di alike? They both like kites, cycling, hiking and climbing.

4. What is Mike designing now? Mike's designing a new style of kite. It's bright shiny lime and glows in the dark incredibly bright.

Spelling and pronunciation practice

The (circled) word in each line has a different vowel sound.

1.	lime	time	white	(with)
2.	kite	sight	(quit)	quite
3.	(still)	smile	style	while
4.	why	sky	(fill)	fly

Pronunciation of words ending with 'ed'

1. 'ed' **not** pronounced as another syllable		2. 'ed' pronounced as another syllable
lived	worked	nodded
played	talked	wanted
loved	dined	delighted
smiled	listened	excited
liked	designed	

Answers - Words with the focus sound in 'H**air** with fl**air** at Mayf**air** Sq**uare**'

1. a flat shape with four sides of equal length — _square_
2. get things ready for something that is planned — _prepare_
3. very unusual, doesn't happen often — _rare_
4. talent or natural ability to do something wonderfully well — _flair_
5. something extra or available for someone to use — _spare_
6. someone who has more than 1,000,000 of their country's currency ($ ¥ £ €) — _millionaire_
7. looking at something for a long time (especially when surprised or thinking) — _staring_
8. having knowledge or information about something — _aware_
9. two things or people connected — _pair_
10. fix something that is damaged, broken or not working correctly — _repair_
11. mother and father — _parents_
12. natural covering of the head — _hair_
13. worried or alarmed about something — _scared_
14. something to sit on; a seat which usually has four legs — _chair_
15. this word shows ownership; means 'belonging to them' — _their_

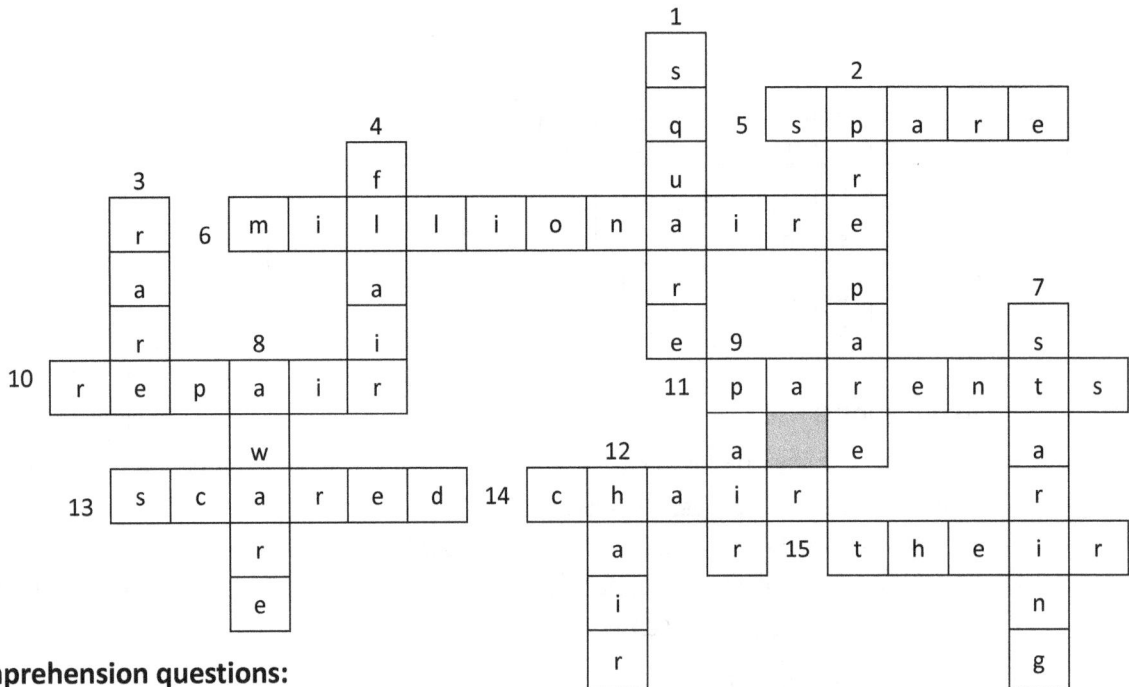

Comprehension questions:

1. What did Sarah and Clare both have a flair for? They had a flair for cutting hair.

2. What did they need to do and buy before they could begin their business?

   They bought square mirrors, as well as square chairs. They bought dryers and combs and six pairs of scissors, They painted the walls with squares and then put signs in the shopping square.

3. What has been the result of their new business? People are coming from everywhere to be 'cut and styled' by Sarah or Clare.

The circled word in each line has a different vowel sound.

1.	pair	fair	chair	(car)
2.	where	(here)	hair	flair
3.	rare	square	(start)	stare
4.	(star)	spare	their	there

Spelling in context – pronouns and contractions

1) We're very happy with our trip. We visited ten countries while we were overseas.
2) You're much taller than your sister but she's older than you, isn't she?
3) We have a new television and it's wonderful. Its best feature is its size.
4) The parents standing over there are very happy because their son graduated
   from university with good results. They're very proud parents.
5) Look! Who's that woman on television?
   She's the woman whose cookbook I've been using.

Spelling - homophones

They're sitting over there and talking about their books.

1. I don't think it's fair that the airfare for the trip has increased again.
2. The boys always stare at each other as they sit on the stair.
3. I don't know where we're going so I don't know what to wear.

Words with 'silent' consonants

silent **w**	silent **k**	silent **b**	silent **g**	silent **l**
write wrong write wrinkle	knee know knew knock	climb thumb comb plumber doubt debt	sign foreign	walk calm palm half calf
silent **t**	silent **s**	silent **n**	silent **h**	silent **g** before **h** or **th**
often listen	aisle isle island	autumn column	rhythm rhyme hour	See page 31 light length right strength

Note: This is not a complete list of all English words with silent letters.

Acknowledgements

Many students, over a number of years, were involved in the trialing process for material used in this resource and though they are too numerous to list, I am grateful to them all.

I would like to thank Matt Thompson for assistance in the pre-print lay-out of the cover for this publication and to Jeanette Christian for proofreading the text. As always, I want to thank my dear husband, Len, for his support and contribution to the production of this book.

Cover images

From left to right: marble carver by Susan Boyer; woman blowing bubbles from Microsoft; man in kayak by Susan Boyer; student with blue background purchased from Fotolia; man in bookstore purchased from photos.com; waitress in coffee shop purchased from photo.com; woman with golden roses by Susan Boyer; chef purchased from Fotolia; painter at easel purchased from photos.com; man looking at painting by Susan Boyer

Photographs, images and graphics used on the content pages:

page 2 - 5:
graphics of banjo, piano, people clapping (p. 3) and other clip art sourced from Microsoft.

page 6 - 11: Jen 'chef' purchased from Fotolia; other images supplied by Microsoft clipart or by Susan Boyer.

page 12 - 17: bubbles and other images supplied by Microsoft clipart.

page 18 - 21: waitress 'Connie', orange tea pot, orange bottle purchased from photos.com; shelf by Susan Boyer; other images sourced from Microsoft clipart.

page 23 photos of mason carving by Susan Boyer.

page 27: Nick, Kim visualising, provided by Microsoft; family having picnic, Nick winking purchased from photos.com; other images by Susan Boyer.

page 28 - 31: graphics sourced from Microsoft clipart

page 33: photos of 'Anouk' and 'Abdul' purchased from photos.com; books sourced from by Microsoft clipart

page 37: photo of, the nurse. purchased from iCLIPART; table with perfume, card and journal by Susan Boyer.
page 38 calendar by Susan Boyer; page 40 – 41 graphics sourced from Microsoft clipart.

page 40: photo of Gina purchased from photos.com; photos of Dino & Nina, skier sourced from Microsoft clipart; other graphics (page 44-45) sourced from Microsoft clipart.

page 49 & 51: balls ,boards & other graphics from Microsoft clipart.

page 53: photo of 'Prue', flutist purchased from photos.com; graphics on page 54 from Microsoft clipart.

page 57: photos of 'Howard' purchased from photos.com; garden fountain by Susan Boyer.
page 61: Kay painting purchased from photos.com; photo of James by S Boyer;
graphics (p. 60 & 63) Microsoft clipart

page 65: Golden roses in vase purchased from photos.com; photo of 'Flo and Joe' supplied by Microsoft
Other images (p. 64 & 67) sourced from Microsoft clipart.

page 69 & 71: tin cans, paper boat and bird sourced from Microsoft clipart.

page 73: 'Mike' the pilot and photo of Di (bottom) purchased from photos.com; other graphics (p. 72 & 74) sourced from Microsoft clipart.

page 77: photo of women looking through window supplied by Microsoft.
Other clipart (p. 76- 80) sourced from Micrsoft clipart; shop sign by Susan Boyer.

www.ingramcontent.com/pod-product-compliance
Lightning Source LLC
Chambersburg PA
CBHW081137090426
42742CB00015BA/2868